SACRED OILS

Sacred Oils

Paul Turner

LITURGICAL PRESS
Collegeville, Minnesota

www.litpress.org

1	2	3	4	5	6	7	8	9

Library of Congress Cataloging-in-Publication Data

Names: Turner, Paul, 1953– author.
Title: Sacred oils / Paul Turner.
Description: Collegeville, Minnesota : Liturgical Press, 2021. | Includes
    bibliographical references. | Summary: "Explores the blessing and
    consecration of the oils at the annual Chrism Mass, as well as the
    guidelines for their usage"— Provided by publisher.
Identifiers: LCCN 2021004719 (print) | LCCN 2021004720 (ebook) |
    ISBN 9780814666449 (paperback) | ISBN 9780814666463 (epub) |
    ISBN 9780814666463 (mobi) | ISBN 9780814666463 (pdf)
Subjects: LCSH: Chrism. | Holy oils.
Classification: LCC BX2047.C5 T87 2021 (print) | LCC BX2047.C5
    (ebook) | DDC 264/.019082—dc23
LC record available at https://lccn.loc.gov/2021004719
LC ebook record available at https://lccn.loc.gov/2021004720

Contents

Chapter Two: The Oil of Catechumens

Chapter Three: Sacred Chrism

Conclusion: The Care of Oils

Abbreviations

AS   Pastoral Care of the Sick: Rites of Anointing and Viaticum (typical edition)

CB   *Ceremonial of Bishops*

CCC   *Catechism of the Catholic Church*

GIRM   The General Instruction of the Roman Missal

OBC   *Order of Baptism of Children*

OBO   *The Order of Blessing the Oil of Catechumens and of the Sick and of Consecrating the Chrism*

OBP   Rites of Ordination of a Bishop, of Priests, and of Deacons

OConf   *The Order of Confirmation*

ODC   *The Order of the Dedication of a Church and an Altar*

PCS   Pastoral Care of the Sick: Rites of Anointing and Viaticum (English edition)

Introduction

The Chrism Mass

Jesus Christ

"Christ" means "Anointed One." The English word comes from the Greek translation of the Hebrew word "Messiah." The Catholic Church incorporates oils into its liturgies to connect the faithful back to the Son of God under this specific title.

In popular prayer, people often call upon the name of "Jesus," a name that means "Savior." In liturgical prayer, he is almost always given a title together with his name: "Lord," "Christ," or both. This practice confirms that believers address their prayers not to a mere historical mortal possessing nothing more than a name, but to the Son of God, who both lived on earth and lives in heaven, whose resurrection affirms his divine title.

The title "Christ" recalls prophecies. Jesus himself on the road to Emmaus catechized his fellow pilgrims by explaining from the scriptures how Moses and all the prophets foresaw that the Messiah, Christ, should suffer the way he did and so enter glory (Luke 24:26-27). The prophecies that the risen Jesus cited that day pertained to his status as the Anointed One.

Those who follow him call themselves "Christians"—disciples of the Anointed One, who themselves have been anointed. The name "Christians" emerged from the ministry of Paul and Barnabas. The newly converted Saul had already been teaching that Jesus was the Messiah (Acts 9:22). The anointing metaphor had captured his imagination and fueled his catechesis. It also energized his opponents. After discovering a plot to take his life, Saul escaped Damascus by hiding inside a large basket that his friends lowered over the city wall. In Jerusalem, he then confronted disciples skeptical of the sincerity of his conversion, until Barnabas took charge of him (Acts 9:27). After that, Paul retreated to his hometown, Tarsus, where, so soon after his conversion and the start of his mission, he surprisingly spent some years in silence (Gal 1:18). Barnabas eventually sought him out and brought him to Antioch (Acts 11:25-26), reigniting Paul's zeal and relaunching his now meteoric mission. Together they spent a year meeting with the local church and educating many people (Acts 11:26). Their teaching in Antioch must have focused on Jesus as the Messiah, which made everyone hunger for an association with him as the Christ. It was then, together with Paul's renewed mission, that the disciples first became known as Christians, a title derived from oil.

All four gospels record that, at some point in Jesus' public ministry, a woman had anointed him. Matthew and Mark say that she anointed his head (Matt 26:7; Mark 14:3). Luke tells of a woman in the house of Simon the Pharisee who anointed Jesus' feet (Luke 7:38). John situates the event six days before Jesus' final Passover in the home of Martha, where the resuscitated Lazarus joined the meal, and Jesus' friend Mary anointed his feet with pure nard (John 12:3). Jesus said that the anointing prepared for his burial. The action confirmed his mortality, and it stirred the belief that he was the Messiah.

After the resurrection, the community of believers recalled those who had gathered against God's holy servant

Jesus, whom God had anointed (Acts 4:27). Peter specifically interpreted the baptism of Jesus as a metaphorical anointing. All four gospels record the baptism, as does Acts of the Apostles in Peter's speech to the household of Cornelius. Although the gospels report no pouring of physical oil at the Jordan River, Peter explained that in that baptism God had anointed Jesus of Nazareth with the Holy Spirit and power (Acts 10:38).

To call Jesus the Anointed One puts him at the end of the line of Old Testament priests, prophets, and kings: The Lord told Moses to anoint Aaron and his sons, consecrating them as priests (Exod 30:30). Aaron's anointed sons enjoyed a perpetual priesthood throughout all future generations (Exod 40:15).

The Lord commanded the prophet Elijah to anoint Elisha as his successor (1 Kgs 19:16). The prophet Isaiah declared how the Lord had anointed him to bring good news to the afflicted (Isa 61:1), a passage that Jesus applied to himself at the synagogue in Nazareth (Luke 4:18).

Samuel poured oil over the head of Saul and declared that the Lord was anointing Saul as king (1 Sam 10:1). Samuel later anointed David, and the Spirit of the Lord rushed upon the new king.[1] Zadok anointed Solomon as king (1 Kgs 1:39).

Jesus is the Christ, the Messiah, the Anointed One, the Priest, the Prophet, and the King. His disciples call themselves Christians to affirm this belief and to share his mission. The Catholic Church assists them with sacred oils.[2]

---

1. 1 Sam 16:13; see also Ps 89:21.

2. See *The Order of Blessing the Oil of Catechumens and of the Sick and of Consecrating the Chrism* [OBO] (Washington, DC: United States Conference of Catholic Bishops, 2019), intro. 2.

Oil

Trees produced the olives, and the olives produced the oil so abundant throughout the Old Testament Mediterranean world. Its production required considerable skill and intense labor. Even though the trees grew well in the local climate, farmers had to care for them, and workers had to harvest the olives. Someone had carry heavy stones to an accessible site. Someone had to fashion them into a mill. Someone had to operate the mill, pressing the olives to release their treasure. Someone had to create flasks and arrange storage space. Someone had to collect the oil and carry it home. Though it often gives pleasure, oil results from hard work.

Olive oil served a variety of purposes. Bakers mixed it with flour. Cooks heated it for meals. Prophets anointed kings. Believers offered it in religious rituals and anointed sacred furnishings. Caretakers filled lamps to provide light. Athletes rubbed it on their bodies to prepare for exercise and to relax after exertion. Perfumers added aromas to fashion cosmetics. Healers applied it to relieve the sick. Mourners anointed the dead.

Today's chefs still favor "extra virgin" olive oil on salads. This first pressing of the fruit produces its "virginal extract." The light texture tastes best at room temperature. Later pressings of the same olives produce oil that heats well for cooking, sautéing, or baking.

In addition to ingesting oil into the body, people rub it onto the body. Topical applications help healing.

The ointment that the Catholic Church traditionally sets aside for religious purposes is olive oil. It immediately links contemporary worship with biblical testimony. As bread and wine are the foundational elements for the Eucharist because of biblical evidence, so sacramental oil has come from a biblically attested source: the olive.

However, evangelization has spread the Gospel beyond the lands where olives grow. Jesus commanded his disciples to teach all nations, and they responded admirably. The Gospel now touches corners of the globe where the expense of shipping olive oil proves burdensome.

Consequently, although the Catholic Church still prefers olive oil for its sacraments, it now allows oil extracted from other plants if that seems appropriate.[3] The term for proper substances in worship is "matter." Plant oil is the matter for anointing in the Catholic Church.

The Code of Canon Law has enshrined the same permission while it cautions not to use old oils.[4] Each year the sacred oils are to be replaced anew.

The production of sacred chrism adds an aromatic source to plant oil. The traditional perfume is the resinous extract drawn from a balsam tree. Today the Catholic Church permits adding any fragrances or aromatic material (OBO, intro. 4). This increases the options for producing the sacred oils necessary for worship.

At its origins, oil was a common product, arduously produced, yet available as widely as bread, wine, and water. Even today, people use oils more than they may realize for food, hygiene, health, beauty, and honor. This common element, devoutly set aside, also performs sacred functions.

---

3. OBO, intro. 3; see also *The Rites*, Pastoral Care of the Sick: Rites of Anointing and Viaticum [PCS], A Pueblo Book (Collegeville, MN: Liturgical Press, 1990), 20.

4. *Code of Canon Law* (Washington, DC: Canon Law Society of America, 1983), 847 §1.

The Day for the Chrism Mass

Each year the bishop of a diocese celebrates a Mass at which he prepares the oils that his priests and deacons will use throughout the year. Although he blesses both the oil of the sick and the oil of catechumens in the same ritual, the Roman Pontifical and the Roman Missal both call the ceremony the chrism Mass, named for the third and most sublime of the oils.

Thursday of Holy Week is the traditional date for the chrism Mass. The rites of initiation at the Easter Vigil require anointings. To provide the freshest of oils for these ceremonies, the bishop presided for this Mass close to that day. Because no Mass may be celebrated on Good Friday or during the day on Holy Saturday, the ceremony defaulted to Holy Thursday. This allowed priests to gather with the bishop that morning for a final Mass during Lent and to obtain the oils that they would need in the parishes for the sacred ceremonies about to come.

However, if it is difficult for the clergy and faithful to gather on the morning of Holy Thursday, the bishop may now celebrate the chrism Mass on an earlier day, still near Easter (OBO 10). Many bishops choose this option, celebrating on a date earlier in Holy Week or even the week prior. They commonly also change the time from morning to evening, when more of the faithful may participate. Celebrating the chrism Mass earlier than Holy Thursday may relieve the demanding preparations for the Sacred Triduum, which begins with the evening Mass of the Lord's Supper, continuing through the observance of Friday of the passion of the Lord, and concluding with the Easter Vigil and the Masses of Easter Sunday. An earlier chrism Mass better allows many people with parish responsibilities to participate in the diocesan event.

In 2020, when the COVID-19 pandemic disrupted the lives of millions, public gatherings ceased out of care for public health. The Vatican's Congregation for Divine Worship and the Discipline of the Sacraments made two statements pertaining to the date of the chrism Mass. On March 19 it stated, "Having evaluated the concrete situation in the different countries, the Bishop has the faculty to postpone it to a later date."[5] Then on March 25 it revised the statement this way: "Evaluating the concrete situation in different countries, the Episcopal Conferences will be able to give indications about a possible transfer to another date."[6] Both versions gave a permission never before expressed: celebrating the chrism Mass at a different time of year, even after Easter. The joy of providing fresh oils for initiation yielded to the charitable responsibility of keeping people safe.

Nonetheless, in a normal year, the celebration of the chrism Mass in the days before the Paschal Triduum gathers representatives of the diocesan church to praise God and pray for those who will be anointed with these oils throughout the coming year.

The Structure of the Chrism Mass

In planning the chrism Mass, a fundamental decision pertains to the sequence of the ceremonies. In its original form, the blessing of the oil of the sick takes place within the eucharistic prayer, just before the final doxology and amen,

5. Decree of the Congregation for Divine Worship and the Discipline of the Sacraments, "In Time of COVID-19," http://www.cultodivino.va /content/cultodivino/it/documenti/decreti-generali/decreti-generali/2020 /decreto-triduo-pasquale-2020.html.
6. Decree of the Congregation for Divine Worship and the Discipline of the Sacraments, "In Time of COVID-19 (II)," http://www.vatican.va /roman_curia/congregations/ccdds/documents/rc_con_ccdds_doc _20200325_decreto-intempodicovid_en.html.

whereas the blessing of the oil of catechumens and the consecration of chrism occur after communion (OBO 11). Alternatively, "for pastoral reasons," the bishop may pray over all three oils in close sequence after the Liturgy of the Word (OBO 12, 26).

This second option makes the ceremony resemble some rituals that may take place during Mass, including confirmations and ordinations. Yet other celebrations, such as baptisms, weddings, and funerals, spread elements of the ceremony throughout the Mass. Some communities have taken the second structural option for so many years that people may not realize that the first option still exists.

One reason why many dioceses choose to combine the prayers over the oils earlier in the Mass is a practical one: Volunteers need time to pour the oils into smaller containers for transport to the local churches. After the consecration of the chrism, they may carry large vessels from the sanctuary to a nearby workspace, leaving behind symbolic smaller vessels for the remainder of the liturgy.

The chrism Mass flows according to one of these two possibilities. Within the chosen structure, other variations arise.

Most noteworthy, when the vessels arrive in the sanctuary, the ministers who carry them announce the names in this order: the oil for the holy chrism, the oil of the sick, and then the oil of catechumens. After each announcement, the ministers place the appropriate vessel on a specially prepared table (OBO 18).

In practice, though, one commonly sees the oils announced in the order in which the bishop will pray over them: the oil of the sick, the oil of catechumens, and then the oil for chrism. Furthermore, although the rubrics envision that the ministers announce the oils and set them in place before the bishop prays over any of them, often they are presented one by one, the bishop's prayer following the announcement and placement of each of the oils. Even the Vatican follows this prac-tice.[7] Perhaps because the ceremony is performed only once a year, its variations stand out in greater relief—both the ones enshrined in the liturgical books and the ones improvised.

The chrism Mass shows one way that the liturgy of the church evolves, accommodating local practices to express divine realities.

The Presentation of the Oils

The oils for Catholic worship are so valued that people formally present them to the bishop within the liturgy of the chrism Mass. First the priests renew their promises, the bishop asks the people to pray for their priests, and they participate in a short litany, which constitutes the universal prayer for this Mass. Then the procession of oils begins.

Deacons and ministers present the oils (OBO 16). If there are no deacons, then priests may assist. They form a proces-sion together with members of the faithful who will carry the gifts for the Mass: the bread, wine, and optionally the water.

Lay ministers may carry the oils designated for the sick and for catechumens, as well as the vessel containing the fragrance. Ordained ministers carry the oil to be consecrated for the chrism. Deacons may carry all of the oil, but including lay people in the procession shows the diversity of ministries in the church and better manifests the entire people of God who benefit from these oils. In some dioceses, those who assist the preparation of adults for initiation, as well as those who prepare parents for the baptism of their children, may carry the oil to be blessed for catechumens and infants. Simi-larly, extraordinary ministers of Holy Communion who bring

7. See, for example, http://www.vatican.va/news_services/liturgy /libretti/2019/20190418-libretto-messa-crismale.pdf, 71–75.

the sacrament to the homebound and hospitalized may carry the oil to be blessed for the sick. These oils will be administered by ordained clergy, but lay people may assist those who anticipate an anointing.

The oils are carried together with the gifts for the Mass. Although many people refer to this as the "offertory procession," its proper title is "procession of the gifts." The "offering" of the Mass happens during the eucharistic prayer. Nonetheless, the inclusion of oil in this procession is unique and significant. Bread and wine are the essential gifts. Water is optional, as are financial contributions for the church and the poor. Other items do not belong in the procession—purificators, corporals, or the finger bowl, for example.

The oils do appear in this procession because they are part of the gifts presented at this Mass. As a celebrant consecrates bread and wine for a sacred purpose in the Mass, so a bishop blesses and consecrates oils. As the bread and wine are fruits of the earth and the work of human hands, so also is oil. The solemn appearance of oil in this procession heightens the anticipation of its future use.

The rubrics say that the ministers present the vessels in this order: first the fragrances, then the oils to be blessed for catechumens and for the sick, and finally the oil to be consecrated for chrism. In those places where the oils are presented one by one immediately before the bishop prays over each, he usually receives the oils for catechumens and the sick first and then the fragrances, just before the oil for chrism.

Nonetheless, the rubrics envision that the fragrances come first, without explaining why. Perhaps they are considered of lesser importance than the oils because they are only an addition. Or perhaps they are extremely important, and their presentation first in the procession anticipates the solemn mixing of chrism.

The prayer after communion for the chrism Mass refers to the fragrances as well as to a verse from the letters of Saint Paul, which calls the community of the faithful "the aroma of Christ to God" (2 Cor 2:15). The bishop prays that those renewed by receiving communion may thereby become "the pleasing fragrance of Christ."[8]

No incense accompanies this procession, which is true in general for the procession of the gifts at any Mass. The bread and wine will be incensed after they have been placed on the altar as a symbol of their offering, and incense will lead the procession of the oils at the end of the Mass to show their sacredness. At the procession of the gifts, the bishop receives ordinary oil along with ordinary bread and ordinary wine, unaccompanied by incense.

The Presider of the Chrism Mass

The bishop of the diocese presides for the chrism Mass. Under certain circumstances, a priest may bless the oils of catechumens and of the sick (OBO 7–8), but the bishop alone consecrates chrism (6). He is regarded as the high priest of the flock (1). He directs the conferring of baptism for his diocese.[9] He is the chief steward of the mysteries of God,[10] the high priest who in turn confers a royal priesthood on the faithful through baptism. Although priests and deacons are also ordinary ministers of baptism, the bishop is the ultimate source of baptismal ministry. Because of his role, the chrism Mass expresses more meaning when members of the faithful fill the cathedral as their bishop presides.

8. Roman Missal, The Chrism Mass 14.
9. Christian Initiation, General Introduction 12.
10. Christian Initiation, General Introduction, referring to 1 Cor 4:1.

Priests and deacons assist the bishop's ministry, so their presence also enhances the chrism Mass. They use chrism when they baptize, they may anoint catechumens and infants, and priests anoint the sick. Their attendance establishes a direct connection between the bishop's prayer over each oil and their administration of it in the sacraments. Especially when priests and deacons anoint with chrism, they hold in their hands a sign of their bishop, the one who was anointed high priest and who directs the conferral of baptism.   .

The Priests at the Chrism Mass

The rubrics urge the priests to concelebrate the chrism Mass with their bishop. Various regions of the diocese are to send representative priests for this purpose (OBO 1). This shows the spread of the bishop's ministry, demonstrates the unity of priests under his leadership, and provides a practical means for priests to secure the oils they need at home. Priests who concelebrate are the bishop's "witnesses and co-workers in the ministry of the sacred Chrism" (OBO 14).

Priests concelebrate more commonly in the era after the Second Vatican Council than they ever did before. People may see concelebrants at events such as funerals or when priests are visiting. Within religious houses, priests may concelebrate at the community's daily Mass. Before the council, concelebration was rare, but it did happen. It existed especially at ordinations, when the newly ordained priests recited the eucharistic prayer together with the bishop, as well as at the chrism Mass. A priest may mistakenly feel as though the chrism Mass is just another concelebration among many others, but he is participating in a long history of a unique permission to concelebrate with a bishop at one of the most solemn occasions of the year.

The physical arrangement of the priests for the oils ceremony indicates the singularity of this celebration. The rubric says that the bishop is "surrounded by the concelebrating Priests" (OBO 22). In ordinary circumstances of concelebration, the priests may surround the altar at the eucharistic prayer. But at this moment, apart from the eucharistic prayer, the priests surround the bishop who conducts the ceremony on another table in the sanctuary.

The Latin expression for the arrangement of the priests with their bishop is *in modum coronæ* (OBO 21). Translators puzzled over how best to express this in English.[11] They considered such options as "like a crown," "on either side," or "in a curved formation." Although "like a crown" is the most literal translation, it sounded more theological than rubrical. In the end, "surrounding" appears in the published book. Nonetheless, the reference to a "crown" in Latin does impart at least a poetic interpretation, if not a theological one. It recalls the Old Testament tradition that among those anointed were kings. The priests arranging themselves like a crown around their bishop suggests that the anointed bishop fulfills a royal role in preparing the oil and that his priests represent a jewel of his ministry.

The Deacons at the Chrism Mass

Deacons are ordinary ministers of baptism, a ceremony in which they administer the oil of catechumens and sacred chrism. Even so, their appearance at the chrism Mass seems more to serve the ceremony of the day than the future

11. The author serves as a facilitator at the meetings of the International Commission on English in the Liturgy (ICEL) and shares personal recollections in passages such as this.

administration of the oils. The priests who concelebrate, by contrast, present an image of unity, witness, and collaboration. Priests show their unity of purpose with the bishop in that they will also administer the oil of the sick on his behalf, and on occasion they will confirm with chrism.

Deacons taking part in the chrism Mass join the entrance procession ahead of the concelebrants (OBO 15). Three of them may have special roles in any celebration with the bishop: two to assist him and one to proclaim the gospel and minister at the altar.[12] Often in practice, a master of ceremonies assists the bishop, and two deacons divide the responsibilities of the Mass, one active through the Liturgy of the Word, and the other prominent through the Liturgy of the Eucharist.

As the ceremony for the oils begins, assisting deacons go to the sacristy or the place where the vessels rest, in order to help carry them (OBO 16). The only vessel that requires the service of a deacon or priest is the one holding the oil to be consecrated for chrism. Lay ministers may carry the others. Still, deacons take a significant part in moving the ceremony forward at this time.

In the sanctuary, as the oils arrive, deacons assist the bishop (OBO 18). The ministers each announce the oil they carry and offer it to the bishop, but deacons place them on the specially prepared table. At a typical Mass, deacons may help receive the gifts of bread and wine and arrange the altar before the priest steps up to preside. So, too, they arrange the gift of the oils that will become part of the solemn exercises to follow.

12. *Ceremonial of Bishops* [CB] (Collegeville, MN: Liturgical Press, 1989), 26.

Deacons practice a threefold ministry: liturgy, preaching, and charity. Many Catholics especially see deacons carry out their liturgical role, vested in stole and dalmatic, at Masses in their parishes. With their words they proclaim the Gospel, they invite the sign of peace, and they command the dismissal; by their deeds they assist with the physical arrangements at the altar of the Eucharist. At the chrism Mass, the liturgical role of a deacon is more complex. His faithful ministry at the altar throughout the year prepares him for his special ministry in the sanctuary on this day. Those deacons who do not have an active role in the sanctuary still vest for the chrism Mass, sharers of the ministry that proclaims the Gospel in word and deed throughout the diocese and under the bishop.

Redeemer

Singing accompanies the procession of the oils. Musicians may lead any suitable song, but the traditional hymn for this occasion carries the Latin title O *Redemptor*, along with this refrain: "O Redeemer, hear your people, as they join in song to you" (OBO 17).

These words appear almost superficial at first. The people who sing them merely identify themselves as the people who sing them. However, they declare that they belong to Christ and that the song is addressed to Christ. The rubric says that a schola or choir sings the verses, but all the people join in the refrain. The full meaning of this hymn requires the vocal participation of the assembly.

The people address Christ as "Redeemer." One might expect people especially at this Mass to address Jesus as the Christ, the Anointed Son of God. However, the assembly calls him "Redeemer," a title that at once evokes the meaning of the birth name Jesus ("Savior") and the purpose of his life to be revealed on Easter Sunday: redemption.

A few prayers at every Mass address Christ, especially around the time for communion; for example, the Lamb of God and the private prayer of the priest before he receives communion. However, most liturgical prayers address the Father through Jesus Christ. The chrism Mass provides a rare example of a hymn addressed to the Second Person of the Trinity.

The halves of each verse rhyme in English, which is not true of the original Latin. ICEL developed this rendering around the time it was translating hundreds of Latin hymns from the Liturgy of the Hours. In that project, the translators agreed *not* to rhyme the stanzas. They feared that each hymn's theological depth would be compromised if they limited the vocabulary to words that rhyme in a proper cadence. The hymn "O Redeemer" shows that ICEL can create rhymes; the challenges here were not as great as in many other hymns.

The verses aptly prepare for the ceremony just beginning. The first verse recalls the trees that provided the oil that the people are now presenting. The nature of those trees, "olive," appears in the second verse. The source of their energy, the sunlight, appears in the first verse. By singing "we present" the oil, the people associate the procession with the presentation of their other gifts for the Eucharist.

The verses then explain the properties of chrism. In baptism it makes "both men and women new" and drives away "all taint of sin." In confirmation "holy gifts come flooding in." One verse says that chrism heals "wounded nature's glory." The word "heals" makes one think that the verse comments on a different oil, that of the sick. But the hymn does not affirm that this oil heals the physical body; rather, it accompanies baptism, which restores the original glory of humanity wounded by sin. Even chrism heals.

Although the church also uses chrism for the ordination of bishops and priests and for the anointing of altars and church walls, the complete focus of this particular hymn— and of most of the chrism Mass—is on the use of chrism in the sacraments of initiation that unify all the faithful followers of Christ, lay and clergy alike.

Each Christian is anointed like Christ, but Christ alone is the Redeemer of Christians. His mission continues every time a follower is anointed with sacred oil.

chapter one

The Oil of the Sick

The Letter of James

Christian anointing of the sick faithfully continues a practice testified to in two New Testament passages. The first of these, the letter of James, offers important details into this prayer of the early church.

James's words still unmask his complex personality. For example, he shows impatience with the rich and those who oppress the poor. Yet he urges those who suffer to show patience with God. In the very same chapter he describes the community's proper outreach to the sick. "Are any among you sick? They should call for the elders of the church and have them pray over them, anointing them with oil in the name of the Lord. The prayer of faith will save the sick, and the Lord will raise them up; and anyone who has committed sins will be forgiven" (Jas 5:14-15).

In two short verses, James discloses precious information. Those who are sick are not thereby helpless. If they have not yet found a physical remedy, they have spiritual resources at the ready. The sick themselves summon the elders of the church. The Greek word for "elders" in this passage is πρεσβυτέρους, which gives English its cognate "presbyters," a group that the Catholic tradition calls its "priests." For James, they possess experience and responsibility. They pray over the sick; that is, they go to the sick person. They are present.

James speaks of "elders" in the plural. He expects a community to have more than one of these respected members and that the group of them will exercise this spiritual duty together.

The elders anoint the sick in the name of the Lord. Oil has healing properties on its own, but James requests something more. He expects the elders to apply it as a sign of the healing properties of the Lord. The Lord heals through the ministry of the elders, a healing represented by anointing.

For James, the prayer and the anointing bring immediate results: The prayer saves the sick, and the Lord raises them up. Those who have committed sins will be forgiven. James expects both a physical and a spiritual healing. He wisely assumes that a sickness of the body conceals a sickness of the spirit. The elders go to the sick in order to address these concerns.

This brief passage reports the inchoate complexities of the early church: membership in a community of believers, the existence of specially designated ministers, the importance of communal prayer for the sick, the use of a material substance to demonstrate God's spiritual power, the concern for both physical and spiritual welfare, the forgiveness of sins, and the need for salvation. Christians have pursued these values in every century.

The Gospel of Mark

The second New Testament passage about anointing the sick gives even briefer testimony yet is especially important because it comes from the gospels and involves the response of the disciples to the command of Jesus.

Having called his twelve disciples, Jesus sent them out in pairs, giving them authority over unclean spirits. They were to travel light, carrying no extra clothing, no bread, and no money. They were to accept hospitality when someone offered it and to shake it off when the locals declined. They preached repentance. Then Saint Mark records this about the ministry of these disciples: They cast out demons and cured many who were sick by anointing them with oil (Mark 6:7-13).

The disciples' use of oil for healing implied that it possessed exorcistic properties. Physical sickness presupposed a spiritual sickness, the presence of some evil spirit taking away the goodness and blessing of health. One way to cure the sick was to expel the responsible demon. If the source of evil lay within the body, a penetrating oil could drive it out. If more evil lurked, hoping to enter, the same oil would erect a protective shield.

This testimony comes from Mark, the earliest of the four gospels. The other evangelists did not report the same apostolic practice. But all of them agreed that Jesus healed the sick, that he desired human wholeness, that he brought people to faith, and that the proclamation of the Gospel included human interaction for the betterment of individuals and of society. When Jesus healed, he sometimes utilized other items and actions: spittle, handlaying, mud and washing; one hope-filled person reached out to touch his garments.[1]

That the disciples anointed the sick shows the desire of Christians to maintain this ministry of Jesus in a style that he personally sanctioned.

---

1. See *Catechism of the Catholic Church* [CCC] 1504, citing Mark 7:32-36; Mark 8:22-25; John 9:6-7; Luke 6:19; Mark 1:41; 3:10; and 6:56.

The Oil of the Sick within the Eucharistic Prayer

At the chrism Mass, the bishop has the option of blessing the oil of the sick inside the eucharistic prayer.[2] This was the custom for many centuries, but the church now offers the option of blessing all the oils after the Liturgy of the Word. That is how many dioceses do it, even though the church permits the earlier tradition.

The practice of blessing within the eucharistic prayer applies only to the oil of the sick, not to the oil of catechumens nor to the sacred chrism.[3] The latter two oils relate to the sacraments of initiation, so they are kept together. The eucharistic prayer includes the consecration of the bread and wine, so a bishop consecrates chrism completely separately, giving proper dignities to both the Eucharist and the sacred oil. For many centuries, the only eucharistic prayer in force was the Roman Canon, now Eucharistic Prayer I, which includes no prayers for those who are not Christian. The eucharistic prayers added to the missal after Vatican II list non-Christians in their intercessions for the living and the dead. In arranging the parts of the original chrism Mass, it probably did not make sense before the end of the canon to pray over an oil to be used for those who had not yet been baptized.

The sick, however, are another matter. The concerns of these faithful Christians remain uppermost in the minds of the church. The Roman Canon prays for members of the living and the dead, as well as for ministers of various ranks. It naturally embraces prayers for the sick.

In some early traditions, the bishop prayed for various goods near the end of the eucharistic prayer, including food-

---

2. OBO 11, 20; Roman Missal, The Chrism Mass 5.
3. See Paul Turner, *Glory in the Cross: Holy Week in the Third Edition of* The Roman Missal (Collegeville, MN: Liturgical Press, 2011), 33–34.

stuffs and oils for families to use. A remnant of that practice may explain the phrase that still appears near the end of Eucharistic Prayer I, "Through [Christ] you continue to make all these good things, O Lord; you sanctify them, fill them with life, bless them, and bestow them upon us." The "good things" mentioned in this prayer may originally have referred to other products that the faithful brought in order to receive a blessing. That context probably explains why the blessing of the oil of the sick appears precisely at that moment of Eucharistic Prayer I, just before the bishop praises God for "these good things." He prays over oil at the moment when previous bishops centuries ago may have prayed over such items as olives and cheese. The conclusions of the other eucharistic prayers make no reference to such objects, yet, if the bishop prays one of them at the chrism Mass, the blessing of the oil of the sick may still take place just before the closing doxology.

The tradition of praying over the oil of the sick within the eucharistic prayer shows the relationship between the substance for the sacrament and the eucharistic bread and wine, as well as the place of the sick within the heart of the church. They may receive the full supplication of the people while the bishop asks God to bless the oil during this sacred moment of the Mass, the eucharistic prayer.

The Father of Consolation

In biblical and Christian tradition, "anointing with oil is a sign of the mercy of God, of the healing of disease, and of the enlightenment of the heart" (CB 644). So wrote the English priest John Cramer (+1848) in his magnificent work connecting quotations from the Greek fathers of Christian antiquity to passages in the New Testament. Commenting on the Gospel of Mark, Cramer showed the full impact of the disciples' ministry when they anointed the sick. This excerpt from Cramer's work so moved the compilers of the Catholic Church's *Ceremonial of Bishops* that they cited it at the beginning of the chapter explaining the particularities that concern the administration of this sacrament when the presider is a bishop.

"A sign of the mercy of God" is the first of the purposes that Cramer ascribes to the oil. Indeed, at the chrism Mass, the central prayer that blesses the oil acclaims the role of the entire Trinity (OBO 20). The Father willed to heal the sick through the Son and now blesses oil through the Holy Spirit. Both this prayer and an alternative form appear in the ritual book for anointing the sick.[4] It treats each member of the Trinity in turn: the Father who sent the Son for salvation, the Son who willed to heal, and the Holy Spirit who strengthens the weak.

In administering the sacrament, if the priest has oil that the bishop has already blessed, he offers a prayer of thanksgiving over the oil, praising the Trinity for the same three reasons (AS 75bis; PCS 123).

As the priest concludes the administration of the sacrament, he may invoke a blessing upon those present (AS 79; PCS 130B). Again, he invokes the entire Trinity, asking the Father to bless, the Son to heal, and the Spirit to shed light.

The prayer of blessing from the chrism Mass opens by addressing God as "Father of all consolation." The entire prayer rests under this title, a fitting echo of Cramer's insight

---

4. *The Rites*, Pastoral Care of the Sick: Rites of Anointing and Viaticum, A Pueblo Book (Collegeville, MN: Liturgical Press, 1990). PCS indicates this English translation; AS indicates the numbering in the typical edition. The prayer from the Chrism Mass is AS 75 and PCS 123; the alternative prayer is AS 242 and PCS 140B.

that this oil signifies the mercy of God. The prayer concludes as the bishop says, "May your holy oil, O Lord, be blessed by you for our sake" (OBO 20). It is God's oil. It is the community's need. God created the oil, and God can repurpose it for the sake of the sick.

Those to be anointed are usually not only sick in body but disquieted in spirit. Losing their former assumptions about life has imperiled their inner peace. They seek consolation, which many people wish to offer. Family and friends extend their support. The medical profession prescribes the aid of treatments, along with a dose of reality. Ultimately, however, the sick seek a deeper consolation, one that relates to the purpose of their being, their enjoyment of life, and their trust in God. God is not merely the Father of consolation, but the Father of *all* consolation. Only God who created each person in mysterious wonder can redeem the person as well. When physical health declines, the promise of eternal life endures. That is consolation.

The Son Who Suffered

In the moments before anointing the sick, the priest leads a brief litany of supplication. One version is addressed to Christ, begging for his mercy (AS 240; PCS 245). It opens with an appeal to him who bore the iniquities and carried the sorrows of those who make this prayer. One hears an echo of the suffering servant from the book of the prophet Isaiah (Isa 53:4), a passage proclaimed in full each year as the first reading for the parish's main celebration on Good Friday of the Lord's passion. The church sees in this passage a prophecy of Jesus, who suffered while redeeming others. By undergoing torment, he identified with the sufferings of all human beings in every age.

The bishop's prayer over the oil puts careful words onto this mystery. He addresses the Father, "who willed to heal the infirmities of the weak through your Son" (OBO 20). The Father did not will the suffering of the Son: the Father willed the healing of infirmities, and the Son's ministry provided the means.

The litany addressed to Christ recalls this ministry. The priest calls him the one so moved with compassion at the crowd that he went about doing good and healing the sick. This evokes Scripture passages such as the miracle of the loaves: Jesus saw the crowds and had compassion on them (Matt 9:36). Peter's catechesis in the house of Cornelius described Jesus as one who went about doing good and healing the sick (Acts 10:38).

The Code of Canon Law says that the church commends the faithful who are dangerously sick to their suffering and glorified Lord so that he may relieve and save them.[5] Through the anointing, the sick connect with Christ who suffered for them and whom the Father raised to glory. Jesus healed the sick as part of his ministry, and he saved all through his paschal mystery. To be sick is to come in touch with the Son who suffered.

The Holy Spirit

When the bishop blesses the oil of the sick at the chrism Mass, he asks God to "send forth from the heavens. . . your Holy Spirit, the Paraclete" (OBO 20). The Scriptures reveal that the heavens are the home of the Holy Spirit in passages such as the baptism of Jesus and Pentecost, the two events that inaugurated the ministries of Christ and the disciples

---

5. Canon 998.

respectively. A new descent of the Spirit upon the oil aids the contemporary church's ministry to the sick.

The bishop calls the Spirit the Paraclete, a title found in several passages from the writings of John. The First Letter of John calls Jesus Christ the Paraclete, the community's advocate with the Father (1 John 2:1). Speaking at the Last Supper, Jesus agreed that the title fit himself as he promised to send "another" Paraclete (John 14:16). The coming of that Paraclete would coincide with Jesus' leaving (John 16:7). Jesus would send the Paraclete from the Father, the spirit of truth who would testify to him (John 15:26). That Paraclete would teach the disciples everything and remind them of all that Jesus told them (John 14:26).

Under this title, Paraclete, the Holy Spirit comes upon the oil of the sick at the bishop's bidding and the Father's kindness. Although the rest of the prayer requests freedom from infirmity, the naming of the Holy Spirit as Paraclete implies something more. The suffering members of the church may be tempted to feel the absence of Christ, so the Father sends the Paraclete to them, the one who will testify to the suffering and glorification of Christ, the one who will teach them and remind them of what Jesus said. In their moments of suffering, the sick will receive catechesis and strength from the Paraclete whom the Father sends from on high.

Human Suffering

A reflection on human suffering opens the introduction to the church's ritual book of anointing and caring for the sick. Sickness is among a person's greatest difficulties, but faith helps one perceive the complete mystery of suffering, which can work toward one's salvation and help one experience the love of Christ, who ministered to the sick throughout his life (AS 1; PCS 1).

People who become sick sometimes wonder if it is their own fault, if some sin of theirs prompted God to punish them. The disciples expressed the same wonderment in John's account of Jesus and the blind man. They asked Jesus whose sin caused the infirmity: that of the man or that of his parents (John 9:3). Jesus replied, "Neither." Sin may not cause suffering at all. Jesus suffered, yet he did not sin. He suffers today alongside his disciples who suffer, and this lightens their afflictions (AS 2; PCS 2).

People fight strenuously against illness in order to regain their roles in human society and in the church (AS 3; PCS 3). Additionally, in the mysterious words of Saint Paul, they make up for what is lacking in the sufferings of Christ (Col 1:24). With this difficult expression, Paul views the continuation of human suffering after the death of Christ as a continuation in the paschal mystery. Human suffering contributes to the view of human redemption. The sick, therefore, have a duty to remind other people about what truly matters and that mortality is redeemed through the cross and resurrection of Christ (AS 3; PCS 3). As the catechism says, "Every illness can make us glimpse death. . . . Very often illness provokes a search for God and a return to him" (CCC 1500–1501). The sick are in partnership with Christ. His sufferings lack nothing that the sick cannot fulfill.

At the chrism Mass, the bishop's prayer over the oil of the sick notes that in general God created plant oil in order "to restore the body." To build upon this natural property, the bishop asks that by the Father's blessing this oil may serve as a "safeguard for body, soul, and spirit." Boldly, he prays that those anointed "may be freed from all pain, all infirmity, and all sickness." This is no small prayer. He is asking that the sick experience physical healing by means of this blessed oil. He seeks their relief in three areas: the pains that result from illness, the infirmity that makes the body susceptible to pain, and the sickness that drives infirmity. In each case, the bishop prays for freedom from "all" of it (OBO 20).

When a loved one becomes ill, a faithful Christian spontaneously offers such a prayer, asking God to relieve the sick of everything that beats them down: all of it.

When a priest prepares to anoint the sick, one of the litanies in the ritual prays for new strength, relief from anguish, deliverance from sin and temptation, life, and salvation (AS 241; PCS 138). Echoing the bishop's bold prayers for healing, the priest carries the message of hope and purpose to the ears of the one who suffers. Some people erroneously hold that the arrival of a priest at the side of the sick signals that all is lost. The contrary is true. He brings the oil that the bishop blessed for healing.

The Minister of Anointing

Only a priest may anoint the sick.[6] Early church history records anointings by others, but the current practice limits the role to priests. Even in the ordination ceremony, the bishop's sample homily reminds the candidates that among the duties they are assuming is to comfort the sick with blessed oil.[7] Before their ordination as priests, they were not qualified to administer this sacrament, not even as deacons.

This restriction probably relates to the biblical testimony in the letter of James. The ministers who anoint the sick are the elders or presbyters of the community (Jas 5:14), an equivalent to today's priests.

---

6. Canon 1003 §1; AS 16; PCS 16.

7. Rites of Ordination of a Bishop, of Priests, and of Deacons [OBP], *The Roman Pontifical* (Vatican City: Vox Clara Committee, 2012), 123.

Some troubled priests resign from ministry and complete a process in which they lose their clerical state to pursue other vocational paths. A priest in this situation is no longer allowed to celebrate sacraments such as anointing the sick. However, if he did anoint someone, the sacrament would be valid because of the permanent effects of his ordination.[8]

Several priests may administer the sacrament to one sick person at the same time (AS 19; PCS 19). All the priests present may lay hands on the sick person. The presider says the prayers and recites the formula while he anoints, but the others may lead the introductory rites, readings, invocations, and invitations. The shortage of priests and the suddenness of some illnesses make it unlikely that this will happen often, but sometimes the sick person has made an impact on the lives of several priests who will come to administer the sacrament together. The provision for several assisting priests does not appear in other liturgical books, such as those for baptism, reconciliation, or matrimony. Its occurrence here surely relates to the same biblical testimony from the letter of James. The writer urges the sick in the community to call upon their presbyters; that is, presbyters in the plural (Jas 5:14). James probably envisioned that they would come as a group. In a similar way, a group of priests may come today.

In a case of necessity, a priest may bless oil that he will use to administer the sacrament.[9] He may not bless oil for a singular ceremony when oil blessed by the bishop is available. However, he may have anointed so frequently that he has exhausted the supply he received after the chrism Mass. Or he may suddenly be asked to anoint when he does not have blessed oil with him. In such a circumstance, a priest may bless the oil that he will use, but only within the cere-

8. See Canon 292 and 1003 §1.
9. AS 21; PCS 21; Canon 999.

mony of anointing; he may not bless it beforehand at a parish church, for example, simply to replenish a diminishing supply. That would look too much like the chrism Mass over which a bishop presides. Instead, within the ceremony of anointing, a priest blesses the oil he will use just before administering it. He uses any plant oil and recites the appropriate prayer, either the same one that the bishop offers at the chrism Mass or its alternative.

If some of the oil he blessed remains after the anointing, he is to absorb it with cotton and burn it in fire (AS 22; PCS 22). This shows both the anomalous nature of the oil he has blessed as well as its sacred property. It is to be reverently and respectfully destroyed.

Although the ministry of anointing is reserved to ordained priests, the ministry of caring for the sick pertains to all. The introduction to the ritual book lists others who have this responsibility: medical professionals as well as those who visit the sick to offer material or spiritual aid (AS 4; PCS 4). In addition to these human agents, Christ himself comes to the aid of the sick through the administration of the sacrament (AS 5; PCS 5). Saint Paul says that those who suffer with Christ will be glorified with him (Rom 8:17). No one who is sick ever suffers alone.

Priests respond generously to requests for anointing, but families and friends of the sick can help by alerting the priest as soon as possible about the illness. Some people wait, thinking that the anointing is only for those who are dying. But the bishop has blessed the oil for its healing properties. Waiting to contact a priest until the sick person is dying is like waiting to contact a doctor until the patient is close to death. By requesting a priest early in an illness, the faithful help him budget his time, and they also provide a means of spiritual and physical solace to the one who is doing everything possible to fight against disease.

When a Bishop Presides

The anointing of the sick is generally carried out by priests, not by bishops (CB 644). A bishop may anoint, of course, but his other responsibilities limit his availability. By blessing the oil and entrusting it to his priests, the bishop takes part in the anointing of all from afar.

The church's reluctance to assign bishops the task of anointing the sick may serve to highlight the occasions when he anoints with chrism: confirmation, ordination, and the dedication of churches and altars. Usage of the oil of the sick generally falls to priests, as anointing with the oil of catechumens usually falls to priests and deacons.

Nonetheless, the bishop is encouraged to preside over communal ceremonies of anointing, such as those relating to a pilgrimage or the gathering of the sick of a diocese (CB 645). In this way he shows his pastoral care for groups of the faithful, not just for private individuals.

The bishop may associate priests with him to assist in administering the sacrament. He imposes hands on at least some of the sick, not necessarily on all of them (CB 653). This is also true when a priest presiding at a large gathering is assisted by other priests (AS 90; PCS 110). In the case of the bishop, the rubric seems to foresee a scenario where the number of sick anticipating an anointing would cause undue delay if the administration of the sacrament required the bishop to pass twice, once to impose hands on each of them, and then again to anoint.

The ritual includes a litany for the sick as well as for those who offer care. As in the case when a priest presides, the bishop may offer the litany either before he lays hands on the sick or after the anointing (CB 652). The anointing ceremony that preceded the reforms of Vatican II had placed the litany after the anointing, but the liturgy now invites the prayers to precede the sacrament, as happens, for example, in baptism. Either sequence is permitted.

After the handlaying during a communal ceremony, the bishop may bless the oil he will use (CB 654). It need not be an emergency for him to do so; he may always bless oil for the sick apart from the chrism Mass, even if a sufficient amount of blessed oil is at hand.

Of course, a bishop may anoint individuals apart from a communal ceremony, as any priest does. He has many ways to show his compassion for the sick.

The Laying on of Hands

Before anointing the sick, the priest lays hands upon them.[10] The reason is clearly biblical. At the end of Mark's gospel, just before the ascension, Jesus gave his disciples some final instructions. Significantly, he commanded them to go into the world to proclaim the Gospel. Jesus promised that certain signs would accompany their ministry. Among these, the disciples should expect the sick to recover after they laid hands on them (Mark 16:18). One of the litanies in the ceremony of anointing the sick recalls this command of Jesus (AS 240; PCS 245).

A laying on of hands accompanies other solemn moments in the church's prayer—confirmation and the ordination of priests, for example. In the baptism of a child, the priest or deacon may place his hand on the child instead of anointing with the oil of catechumens. A priest raises his hand to offer the words of absolution in confession. He extends his hands over the offerings at Mass to pray for the coming of the Holy Spirit to change the bread and wine into the Body and Blood

---

10. AS 5 and 74; PCS 5 and 122, for example.

of Christ. The gesture generally implies a blessing or prayer for the coming of the Holy Spirit. In the case of the sick, the bishop's prayer of blessing at the chrism Mass asks God to send the Paraclete upon the oil. This gift of the Holy Spirit may be recalled every time a priest imposes hands on the sick person's head.

When many priests come for the anointing of an individual, they may each join in handlaying (AS 19; PCS 19). Only one of them anoints, but all may exercise their ministry in this way. Handlaying is important but ancillary.

While imposing hands upon the sick, a priest says nothing (AS 74; PCS 122). The gesture alone evokes the complete meaning of this ceremony. He gives no verbal catechesis to the sick person, no aural prayer to God. He lets the gesture speak.

When he anoints a group of people, the priest is to impose hands on each (AS 67; PCS 110). If several priests are present for the anointing of a large group, each priest lays hands on and anoints some of the group (AS 90; PCS 110). Implicitly, he anoints the same people upon whom he laid hands.

The rubrics do not give a priest the option of extending his hands over the entire group, probably because of Jesus' specific instruction at the end of Mark's gospel to lay hands on the sick. However, in a case where contagion is a danger, or the priest may not have access to the sick person's head, or the number of the sick is excessive, an extension of hands seems a logical option. After all, in extreme cases, the priest may omit the handlaying altogether and simply anoint in danger of an imminent death (AS 116; PCS 237, 261).

The handlaying is omitted when the sick person is to be confirmed in the same ceremony (AS 117, 124; PCS 238, 246). Confirmation includes a laying on of hands, and the combined liturgy avoids a duplication of the gesture. This circumstance reinforces that the handlaying for anointing is expressive but not essential for the sacrament. Still, it conveys a powerful symbol: the invocation of the Holy Spirit.

Oil "from the Verdant Tree"

There can be no oil without some kind of plant, and the prayer of blessing over the oil praises God who "graciously brought forth [the oil] from the verdant tree" (OBO 20).

ICEL struggled to find the right translation for this phrase. In Latin, it is *de viridi ligno*. The translators offered "from the green tree," but this seemed unimportant information in the context of the prayer. Trees are usually green.

Someone proposed "from the green wood" because of the biblical allusion to the passion of Christ. Jesus cited a proverb to the wailing women: "If they do this when the wood is green, what will happen when it is dry?" (Luke 23:31). But that mysterious saying seemed not to apply to the prayer at hand. Besides, olives come from a tree, not from wood.

"From the healthy tree" was also proposed, but that seemed too limited a translation, even for a blessing of oil for the sick.

At first, "from the verdant tree" did not find favor because it sounded more like something one would find in a pasture than in an olive orchard. Nonetheless, "verdant" remains in the final translation. After all, the church no longer limits a bishop to bless oil that comes from olives, even though they still provide the common source.

At times, it is hard to find the right word that honors a prayer's long tradition and yet applies to contemporary realities. Seemingly identical words carry different shades of meanings when they move from one language to another.

This can be said of the same sickness that may afflict different people with symptoms of different strengths. It is hard to find the right medicine, the right care, and the right words. Still, every expression of care conveys the same message: The church prays for healing, and the church believes that healing comes from Christ, whose care produces fruit, like a verdant tree.

Anointing Parts of the Body

The priest spreads oil on the forehead and on the hands of the sick (AS 23; PCS 23). However, there may be exceptions.

At times, he may anoint in this way only with difficulty. Perhaps the group of the sick is unusually large, or the sick person is in such danger that the priest must move quickly. Or the priest may not have access to the sick person's hands due to bandaging, covering, or the distance he must keep. He may then anoint only the forehead. At other times, he may not even have access to the forehead. In those cases, he may anoint any part of the body.[11] In all circumstances, he says the complete formula.

The ritual book does not specify what part of the hands to anoint. In practice, a priest usually anoints the palms, but his instructions only say "hands."[12] Before the post-Vatican II liturgical reforms, the priest anointed the sick on the palms unless the sick person was another priest. Then the ministering priest anointed the back of the sick priest's hands. The custom showed deference to the previous anointing of palms, done with chrism, which the ailing priest had received at his ordination. If a sick priest were to request anointing on the back of his hands today, he may receive it that way, but it is not required. The oils are different, and they serve different

11. Canon 1000 §1.
12. AS 23 and 76; PCS 23 and 124, for example.

purposes. In another example, the baptism of a child includes an anointing with chrism on the forehead, yet the anointing with the oil of the sick on the same forehead years later causes no confusion of purpose. Indeed, a priest may anoint a layperson on the back of the hands, especially if only that part of the hand is accessible to him.

Typically a priest anoints from an oil stock, a small metal container holding a cotton ball soaked with blessed oil. He unscrews the lid, presses his thumb into the cotton, and anoints with the oil that clings. He reuses the same stock for many anointings.

However, a priest may use an instrument to anoint the sick; he need not use his thumb.[13] This permission is granted for unspecified serious reasons. The most obvious is danger of contagion. Either the sick person or the priest could contract an illness from the other. In such danger, the priest would wisely use a cotton swab or a single-use cotton ball. He then appropriately places the used instrument inside a separate container such as a metal vessel or plastic bag. It is best burned after the anointing, similar to the burning of leftover oil that a priest has blessed in a case of emergency (AS 22; PCS 22). The use of instruments became more common in 2020 amidst the pandemic.

The Formula for Anointing the Sick

As the priest anoints, he usually recites the sacramental formula in two parts. While anointing the forehead, he says, "Through this Holy Anointing may the Lord in his love and mercy help you with the grace of the Holy Spirit." Then, while anointing the hands, he says, "May the Lord who frees

---

13. Canon 1000 §2.

you from sin save you and raise you up." The sick person responds "Amen" to each part of the formula.[14]

In practice, the priest may need to instruct the sick person; for example, "I will anoint your forehead and the palms of your hands. Please answer 'Amen' each time." Otherwise, the sick may not know what to say or when. At times, the person is too sick to respond. The priest continues anyway.

In Latin, these two phrases connect one long sentence, interrupted by the first "Amen." The second half is the hoped-for result of the first: The priest prays for the grace of the Holy Spirit *so that* the Lord who frees from sin may save and raise up the sick.

The formula shows the centrality of the Holy Spirit in this prayer. It recalls both the bishop's prayer of blessing at the chrism Mass, when he asked for the gift of the Paraclete upon the oil, and the laying on of hands that just preceded the anointing. The priest calls upon the healing power of the Holy Spirit, the Paraclete active in the church.

The prayer explicitly intercedes for "help." That help is explained as salvation and a raising up: a spiritual healing and a physical healing. These purposes directly relate to the letter of James, which states that the prayer of the presbyters will save the sick and that the Lord will raise them up (Jas 5:15). In truth, the meaning of that verb is ambiguous. Does it mean that the Lord will "raise" the sick from prone to upright, or from death to life? Both can be inferred from the letter and from the church's liturgy. Nonetheless, because the bishop has asked God to bless the oil for the purposes of physical healing, that meaning cannot be excluded from the sacramental formula.

14. AS 76; PCS 124, for example.

In the ordination rite, the bishop's sample homily instructs the candidates for priesthood that their ministry will include coming to the aid of the sick. The Latin word there, *sublevantes*, is related to the word *allevet* that appears in the formula for anointing the sick. The ordination homily foresees that priests will come to the aid of the sick in the manner that the letter of James envisioned: raising them up.

As a priest begins the ceremony of anointing the sick, he cites the same letter in order to explain his purpose (AS 70; PCS 117). He first recalls how Jesus healed the sick in his ministry and suffered affliction at the end of his life. He then quotes the words of James, who urged the sick to summon the priests. Alternatively, the priest may address these sentiments not to the people gathered around him, but in a prayer to God.[15] Either way, his very introduction to the ceremony prepares for the formula that will link the testimony of James with the sacrament of the sick.

Eligible Illness

Those eligible to receive the anointing of the sick fall into various categories. The most common is those who suffer a serious illness. In the past, this sacrament was known as Extreme Unction or Last Anointing. It formed part of the church's care for the dying. Now the church positions the anointing within its pastoral care of the sick. Anyone with a serious illness is eligible, even if it is not terminal.

The bishop's prayer at the chrism Mass describes those who will benefit from this oil. He recalls that God willed to heal "the infirmities of the weak." Then he prays that the oil

15. AS 239; PCS 155, where this is included only in the visit to a hospital or institution.

may be "a safeguard for body, soul, and spirit," and that those who are anointed may be freed "from all pain, all infirmity, and all sickness" (OBO 20). The prayer distinguishes infirmity and weakness. Some people are weakened by age, which increases their chance of infirmity. The prayer covers these situations.

Those who are eligible, then, are those who are seriously ill because of sickness or age (AS 8; PCS 8). In individual cases, the church asks for a prudent and probable judgment on the gravity of the illness (AS 8; PCS 8). For example, those preparing for surgery because of a serious illness are eligible (AS 10; PCS 10). Although this does not automatically apply to elective procedures, some presurgery counsel and paperwork aim to prepare the infirm for the worst should some tragedy result. If even an elective surgery puts the patient's life in danger, a prudent spiritual judgment may determine that this patient is eligible for anointing.

Those who are unconscious may also be eligible. The same is true for those who have lost the use of reason, likely through dementia. If with better mental capacities they would have requested the anointing, they may receive it when incapable of stating the request.[16]

Regarding persons with disabilities, the bishops of the United States have clarified their eligibility: "Since disability does not necessarily indicate an illness, Catholics with disabilities should receive the Anointing of the Sick on the same basis and under the same circumstances as any other member of the Christian faithful."[17] The presence of a disability there-

---

16. AS 14; PCS 14; Canon 1006.

17. Guidelines for the Celebration of the Sacraments with Persons with Disabilities, rev. ed. (Washington, DC: United States Conference of Catholic Bishops, 2017), 34.

fore does not always call for an anointing. As with other members of the community, those who are disabled may instead pray for those who are sick.

A person may receive the anointing more than once if, having recovered, the previous condition returns, or, without recovery, if the condition worsens.[18] Some whose age has made them more susceptible to weakness take advantage of the anointing whenever a priest is available. This alleviates a reasonable concern that a priest may not be available should their condition suddenly intensify.

Eligible Non-Catholic Christians

A validly baptized Christian who is not a member of the Catholic Church may be eligible for the sacrament of the anointing of the sick by a Catholic priest. The legislation appeared in the Code of Canon Law[19] and is repeated in the Vatican's 1993 Directory for the Application of Principles and Norms on Ecumenism.[20]

Roman Catholics who do not have access to their own priest may receive the sacrament from an Eastern Rite priest,[21] and those who belong to Eastern Rites without access to their own priest may receive the sacrament from a Latin Rite Roman Catholic priest.[22]

---

18. AS 9; PCS 9; Canon 1004 §2.

19. Canon 844.

20. Pontificium Consilium ad Christianorum Unitatem Fovendam, Directory for the Application of Principles and Norms on Ecumenism, http://www.vatican.va/roman_curia/pontifical_councils/chrstuni/documents/rc_pc_chrstuni_doc_25031993_principles-and-norms-on-ecumenism_en.html.

21. Directory for the Application of Principles 123.

22. Directory for the Application of Principles 125.

A Catholic priest may administer the sacrament of the sick to a Christian of another community, such as a member of a Protestant congregation, under certain conditions: "that the person be unable to have recourse for the sacrament desired to a minister of his or her own church or ecclesial Community, ask for the sacrament of his or her own initiative, manifest Catholic faith in this sacrament, and be properly disposed."[23]

All these conditions matter. The sick may not have access to a minister of their own denomination, or perhaps that community of believers does not practice anointing. The sick need to ask for the sacrament of their own free will: No one is forcing them, and if they are unconscious, someone has to attest to their presumed desire. Additionally, the sick person has to share the Catholic faith in the sacrament, that the Lord relieves and saves the sick through its administration.[24] The person should also be properly disposed, having been catechized in the meaning of the ceremony and spiritually ready for its celebration.

If a person is in danger of death, a priest may anoint after making this judgment on his own. Otherwise, it is strongly recommended that the diocesan bishop establish the norms for judging these situations.[25] He may entrust a nonemergency decision to his priests, or he may reserve the judgment for himself.

The same criteria exist for the administration of the sacraments of the Eucharist and penance.[26] At times the Catholic Church not only permits but commends the sharing of sacra-

---

23. Directory for the Application of Principles 131.
24. For example, Canon 998; CCC 1499.
25. Directory for the Application of Principles 130.
26. Directory for the Application of Principles 131.

ments with other Christians. This can provide a source of comfort for the entire community of faith.

Eligible Age

People of advanced age are eligible to receive the anointing even if they have no apparent serious illness (AS 11; PCS 9). As long as their strength has been weakened by age, they may receive the sacrament. The church sets no predetermined number of years as one's "advanced age." Obviously, an anointing is not intended to reverse one's age but to strengthen the weakness that age can bring.

The ritual book includes a prayer after anointing specifically for the person who has reached advanced age. It recognizes the elderly person's appeal for health in body and soul, and it prays that their faith and hope may offer others an example of patient suffering and the joy of God's love (AS 243; PCS 243).

At the other end of the spectrum, children who face a serious sickness become eligible to be anointed once they have reached the use of reason, not before.[27] For First Communion, this is commonly understood to be about the age of seven, but again the church does not set a predetermined number of years to define "use of reason."

The ritual book allows a priest to anoint children if they have enough reason to be comforted by it (AS 12; PCS 12). This differs from the explanation for First Communion, when a child becomes eligible with the understanding of the difference between ordinary food and eucharistic food.[28] "Reason" in the case of anointing pertains to spiritual com-

---

27. Canon 1004 §1.
28. Canon 913 §2.

fort. In case of doubt that a child has such reason, the sacrament may be conferred.[29] Parents will be good judges of the awareness of their children.

Not Anointing Infants

Infants have not attained the use of reason and are therefore not eligible to receive the anointing of the sick.[30] This restriction puzzles many parents of a sick infant. They would like the church to use the full power of the sacraments for a helpless child. After all, the church defends the sacredness of all human life, even in the womb.

Originally, when the anointing was reserved for the dying, this provision probably related to the power of this sacrament to forgive sins. Children younger than the age of reason are not capable of serious sin and, therefore, do not need the forgiving properties of an anointing. Still, the ritual prays for the healing of the body, not just of the spirit. The disquiet felt by many parents of ill infants represents their belief in the healing powers of the sacrament of the anointing of the sick.

Although the church does not permit priests to anoint infants, it does permit baptism and even confirmation if the infant is in danger of death. Infants may not receive communion, a restriction that most Catholic parents accept without question. Anointing is primarily for the one who can experience its comfort—the sick person, not the sick person's parents and caregivers.

If a priest were to anoint an infant, the sacrament would be valid, though canonically illicit. Still, the church holds

29. AS 12; PCS 12; Canon 1005.
30. Canon 1004 §1.

that other sacramental helps and prayers more appropriately assist its youngest ailing members.

Not Anointing Those in Serious Sin

Canon law forbids a priest to anoint those who obstinately persist in manifestly serious sin.[31] Some people are public sinners. Their misbehavior is well known. They have widely announced their disrespect for the church, its sacraments, and its morals—sometimes on social media platforms. The community of the faithful could experience understandable dismay if a priest were to administer a sacrament to a person who held such positions.

Nonetheless, Christians acknowledge the possibility of repentance. The final judgment of a person's soul is difficult to perceive. A priest may be summoned to hear the repentance of a sinner and then be bound by silence not to divulge the confession. He may end up anointing someone whom others presume persists in sin.

Without repentance, a serious sinner is not eligible to receive any of the sacraments, including the anointing of the sick.

Not Anointing Those To Be Confirmed

At times the priest learns that the person he has come to anoint is in danger of death and has never received the sacrament of confirmation. He confirms this person before saying the prayers for the dying (AS 31; PCS 31), and he does not ordinarily give the anointing of the sick.

---

31. Canon 1007; AS 15.

However, if the person survives the danger, and if the illness returns, the priest may offer the anointing. The church discourages administering both anointings in one continuous rite, not the celebration of the two sacraments on separate occasions.[32]

Separating the sacraments avoids confusion between the anointings. The minister imposes hands and anoints the forehead in both rituals, although he may administer the oil of the sick on another part of the person's body (AS 117; PCS 238).

If it is necessary to give both anointings, confirmation with its handlaying and anointing comes first. Then the handlaying associated with the anointing of the sick is omitted (AS 117, 124; PCS 238, 246). This avoids the repetition of the same gesture while affirming the distinct purposes of the oils.

When a person is in danger of death, the church stands ready to offer appropriate prayers and sacraments. Difficult decisions face the ministers who extend comfort, hope, prayer, and the correct use of the church's sacred oils.

Not Anointing the Dying and the Dead

Those who have died are not eligible for the anointing (AS 15; PCS 15). They have already passed from this life. Sacramental signs no longer apply.

If a doubt persists that the person has died, the priest may anoint.[33] The ritual book contains a brief service. The priest invites others to pray, and then he anoints with the usual formula (AS 135; PCS 268–69). In the past, a priest in this

---

32. *The Order of Confirmation* (Washington, DC: United States Conference of Catholic Bishops, 2016), "Confirmation to Be Administered to a Sick Person in Danger of Death," 52.

33. Canon 1005; AS 15; PCS 15.

situation used a conditional formula such as, "If you are alive, through this holy anointing, may the Lord in his love and mercy help you. . ." But now he simply offers the normal formula. The condition is left implicit.

The church offers other ceremonies after death. A priest who arrives too late to anoint may still lead the prayers for the dead contained within the same ritual book (AS 145–51; PCS 219–21). These more appropriately apply to the circumstances of death. They pray for the forgiveness of the person's sins and for the admission of the deceased into the eternal kingdom of God.

If the priest arrives while the person is dying, he makes a judgment on the appropriateness of anointing. If prayers for healing no longer apply, if the person and the family have accepted that death is imminent, and if the person has already been anointed, the priest justifiably does not anoint the dying person again. Instead, he leads those with him in the commendation of the dying (AS 138–51; PCS 213–21).

In the absence of a priest, a deacon or a layperson may offer the same commendation (AS 142; PCS 213). The church is so anxious to assist faithful members at this time that it provides a ceremony that anyone may lead, following the official prayers in the ritual book. Such "elders" or respected members of the community may not anoint, but in partial imitation of the elders in the letter of James, they may pray at the side of the sick.

Many people assume that as death draws near to a person they know, they should contact a priest. However, these prayers of commendation at the time of death do not require the presence of an ordained minister.

Only a priest gives absolution to a penitent, but the one who is dying may have lost the ability to confess. A priest may impart the apostolic pardon after confession, but the church confers this plenary indulgence even on a faithful

Catholic who dies without a priest present.[34] Only a priest may anoint, but the time for anointing has probably passed.

Anyone may lead the prayers for the dying, and any deacon or extraordinary minister of Holy Communion may offer viaticum. A good pastor will want to come to the bedside of a dying member of his flock, but he will also train other people, so that they too may bring the consolation of the church at this crucial time.

The intensely beautiful service of commendation focuses the attention of all on the sacred moment at the end of one human life. To begin, all may repeat short biblical formulas after the minister. Someone may then read a longer passage. All may pray the litany of the saints, concluding the invocations not with "pray for us" but with a specific prayer for the one who is dying: "pray for him" or "pray for her" (AS 145; PCS 219).

The minister then chooses one or more options from a suite of orations. The first of these is one of the boldest prayers in all the liturgical books. The minister commands the dying soul to go forth from this world into the next (AS 146; PCS 220A). Other prayers may follow after the person has died.

There need not be an anointing at the time of death. The sacred oil of the sick may have already done all it can do.

Anointing and Viaticum

When a person is in danger of death, the sacrament the church most wants to share is Holy Communion under the

---

34. Enchiridion on Indulgences, Other Grants of Indulgences 28, The Moment of Death, https://d2y1pz2y630308.cloudfront.net/15471/documents/2016/10/Sacred%20Apostolic%20Penitentiary-The%20Enchiridion%20of%20Indulgences.pdf.

form of viaticum, a word that implies food for the journey (AS 93; PCS 176). The dying faithful who are able to receive communion are actually bound under obligation to receive viaticum (AS 27; PCS 27). If a priest or deacon is not available, any duly appointed extraordinary minister of Holy Communion may conduct the ceremony (AS 29; PCS 29).

The phrase "last rites" remains common in society, but the ritual book for anointing of the sick never uses it. People commonly think that they need a priest to administer last rites when a Catholic is dying. They actually need any communion minister at a time early enough in the process of dying that the person in question may receive viaticum.

A priest may anoint the sick at any point of the illness, and the moment of death is often not the appropriate time. Only a priest can hear confessions, but a confession can usually be arranged well in advance of the time of dying. Viaticum is the most important last rite.

If the person has not been anointed recently, it may be appropriate for a priest to conduct the continuous rite of anointing and viaticum (AS 30; PCS 30). He may hear the confession of the sick person and then give the plenary indulgence that the church offers at the moment of death (AS 121–22; PCS 242–43). The priest leads the dying person in the renewal of baptismal promises. In unusual circumstances he administers confirmation. Then he proceeds with the anointing of the sick. After all recite the Lord's Prayer, the priest gives communion as viaticum and concludes the rite.

Viaticum may be administered without the other sacraments when appropriate. The continuous rite shows the relative significance of the sacraments. The dying are entitled to an anointing, but it may be omitted. More important is that a representative of the church comes while the dying person is still conscious enough to renew baptismal promises and capable enough to swallow communion under either form of bread or wine. Then the person who ideally has already been anointed one or more times receives the proper last rite: viaticum.

chapter two

The Oil of Catechumens

Strength

When the bishop blesses the oil of catechumens at the chrism Mass, he calls God by the title "strength," and he declares that God created oil as "a sign of strength." He also calls God the "protection" of his people (OBO 22).

In the very opening lines of the blessing, the bishop declares to God how defenseless people are without divine aid. This oil, which is destined exclusively for those who have not yet been baptized, signifies the strength that God alone can give those in spiritual weakness due to the power of the devil over anyone not yet fortified with the grace of the sacraments. In earlier times, this was called the oil of exorcism.

The use of the word "strength" recalls a passage from the book of Psalms. While praying in thanksgiving over enemies, the believer marvels, "You give me the strength of a wild ox; you have poured out on me purest oil" (Ps 92:11, Abbey Psalms and Canticles). God's oil provides overpowering strength against the foe. An agrarian society that found the power of wild oxen a wonder to behold stood in awe that God offered the same power to humans engaging in conflict. Catechumens will receive that kind of strength in their struggle to convert from a life without Christ to full discipleship.

When catechumens are anointed, the bishop continues, they will receive courage, divine wisdom, and power to understand the Gospel more deeply, take on the responsibilities of the Christian life, and eventually rejoice in the new birth of their baptism (OBO 22).

Through baptism, the bishop explains, God will adopt catechumens as sons and daughters. The New Testament says as much. Saint Paul told the Galatians that through faith they were children of God in Christ Jesus (Gal 3:26). Paul repeated the image in his letter to the Romans. Adopted children may call God their Father and receive a joint inheritance with Christ the Son of God (Rom 18:14-17).

The oil of catechumens provides strength to those enduring spiritual battles on the journey toward life in Christ.

Opting In

The Vatican permits conferences of bishops to determine whether or not to include the oil of catechumens in the ceremonies prior to the baptism of adults and children (OBO 7). After Vatican II, the group responsible for implementing the changes in the liturgy considered omitting the blessing of the oil of catechumens from the chrism Mass. They reasoned that it could become optional in the baptism of infants, and a priest could be authorized to bless it, making the bishop's blessing unnecessary.[1] In the end, the optional blessing of this oil remains in the chrism Mass, its inclusion determined not by the Vatican nor by any single bishop, but by his conference.

---

1. Paul Turner, *Glory in the Cross: Holy Week in the Third Edition of The Roman Missal* (Collegeville, MN: Liturgical Press, 2011), 34.

Both ritual books for initiating adults and baptizing children include a section of adaptations that conferences of bishops are permitted to make. Among these remains the option to omit entirely the anointing with the oil of catechumens.[2]

Consequently, at the chrism Mass, the rubric pertaining to this oil says the bishop proceeds with it "if it is to be blessed" (OBO 21). If the conference of bishops decides not to include this oil in its catechumenal and baptismal rituals, then the chrism Mass features only two oils: the oil of the sick and chrism.

The United States Conference of Catholic Bishops opts in. However, it remands the decision to anoint infants to the priest or deacon who performs the baptism. The anointing of catechumens may take place during the period of the catechumenate sometime before the Rite of Election (OCIA 132; RCIA 103). The conference has decided that the oil has sufficient merit to include it as an option in the ritual books.

Chrism Mass Alternatives

At the chrism Mass, the bishop may bless the oil of catechumens either after communion or after the procession of the gifts. The first option comes from the pre-Vatican II tradition, in which the blessing of the oil of catechumens came last, following the consecration of chrism, as if the oil of catechumens were of least importance. Today, although the bishop may still pray over both these oils after

---

2. OCIA 65:7; RCIA 33:7. "OCIA" refers to the numbering in the typical edition in Latin; "RCIA" refers to the 1988 English translation of the *Rite of Christian Initiation of Adults* (Collegeville, MN: Liturgical Press, 1988). *Order of Baptism of Children* [OBC] (Collegeville, MN: Liturgical Press, 2020), 24:2.

communion, the blessing of the oil of catechumens always precedes the consecration of chrism, whether after the procession of the gifts or after communion. This probably suggests that the prayers reach a climax with chrism, the greatest of the three oils.

The oil of catechumens always appears in relationship with the oil of chrism. Praying over these two oils after communion, completely apart from the oil of the sick, shows their distinctive usage. The first oil pertains only to those faithful Christians who are sick, whereas the other two pertain to the initiation rites. When the bishop prays over these two oils near the end of the chrism Mass, they almost immediately join the procession out of the cathedral, destined for the parishes.

Alternatively, praying over the oil of catechumens earlier in the chrism Mass shows its connection to other sacraments, both in the preparation of oils that several sacraments share in common and in their liturgical usage, commonly celebrated at Mass after the Liturgy of the Word.

Minister

An ordained priest or deacon administers the oil of catechumens. The anointing is always optional, but the minister must be a priest or a deacon (OCIA 127; RCIA 98). In the 1988 English translation of the RCIA, this seemed ambiguous. Referring to the oil of catechumens, it stated, "The presiding celebrant for such a first anointing of the catechumens is a priest or a deacon" (RCIA 98). Then it stated that "this rite of anointing may be celebrated several times during the course of the catechumenate."[3] Understandably, this

3. RCIA 100; see OCIA 127 and 128.

made some wonder if a layperson could anoint catechumens on subsequent occasions after a priest or deacon conducted the first anointing of a series. However, the ritual calls this the first anointing to distinguish it from the anointing with chrism that will follow at their initiation.

The Order of Baptism of Children includes a ceremony to be led by a deputed lay minister in parts of the world where clergy are scarce. Because that minister has not been ordained, anointing with the oil of catechumens is omitted (OBC 140).

If the priest does not have a supply of this oil blessed by the bishop, he may bless his own to anoint an adult catechumen, but not to anoint an infant (OBC 51). For example, the parish may have exhausted its supply, or the priest is anointing a catechumen privately at some distance from the stored oil.

A deacon, however, may not bless his own oil to anoint a catechumen.[4] If there is no oil, and there is no priest, then there is no anointing.

More than one minister may anoint if the group of catechumens is large (OCIA 130; RCIA 103). A priest may even be assisted by a deacon. The same permission applies to anointing during the baptism of children (OBC 50).

When a bishop presides for the baptism of an infant, if the child is to be anointed with the oil of catechumens, the preferred minister of anointing is a priest, usually the pastor. The same priest performs other auxiliary ceremonies, such as the postbaptismal anointing, the clothing with the baptismal garment, the giving of the lighted candle, and the *Ephphetha* (CB 432, 439, and 444). This minimizes the potential confusion resulting from an anointing by a bishop. The bishop

---

4. OCIA 129; RCIA 101; OBO 7.

usually anoints with chrism at confirmation and ordinations. The anointing with the oil of catechumens is best carried out, then, by another ordained minister. In the case of adults, the bishop may anoint catechumens during the period of the catechumenate (CB 407).

Occasion for Anointing Catechumens

A conference of bishops not only has the freedom to omit completely the administration of the oil of catechumens, it may assign the anointing of catechumens at different stages of their formation. For example, it may be offered as a rite of passage throughout the period of the catechumenate, as part of the preparation rites on Holy Saturday, or during the Easter Vigil between the renunciations and the profession of faith.[5]

A priest or deacon may anoint catechumens within a celebration of the Word of God during the period of the catechumenate (OCIA 128; RCIA 100). Such a celebration may take three different forms: It may gather the catechumens on a Sunday morning for their own spiritual formation apart from the full community; it may involve the catechumens in the Liturgy of the Word at the community's Sunday Mass; or it may be held in conjunction with a catechumenal session, not necessarily on a Sunday (OCIA 107–8; RCIA 83–84).

Catechumens may receive an anointing individually apart from the group if this seems pastorally advisable. They may also be anointed more than once if circumstances suggest (OCIA 128; RCIA 100). Because some catechumens spend years in formation, advancing from one stage to another, an anointing may mark such ritual passages throughout their years of preparation (OCIA 103; RCIA 79).

---

5. OCIA 65 §§6, 7; RCIA 33 §§6, 7.

In parishes, then, catechumens may be anointed privately, within a group meeting, or at the Sunday Mass, once or several times throughout their formation.

Universally, another anointing with the oil of catechumens may take place on Holy Saturday,[6] but only with the approval of the conference of bishops. The anointing fittingly occurs during the Easter Vigil between the renunciations and the profession of faith, as indicated in the Roman Missal (48). However, in order to save time at the Vigil, the anointing may be administered earlier on Holy Saturday as part of the preparation rites (OCIA 206, 212; RCIA 99). Traditionally, a catechumen received the anointing before reciting the Creed, which is still a possibility for the elect. It serves as a final prayer of exorcism, sealing out whatever might keep the elect from professing their faith in the triune God. However, it may be administered after reciting the Creed, in order to confirm it.[7] The prebaptismal anointing of adults with the oil of catechumens shows their need for divine strength: forsaking the past and overcoming the power of the devil, they confidently profess their faith and hold to it throughout their lives (OCIA 212; RCIA 99).

In the United States, however, the conference of bishops decided not to include the anointing with the oil of catechumens on Holy Saturday or at the Easter Vigil.[8] This limits its administration to the period of the catechumenate and the period of purification and enlightenment, which usually coincides with Lent. Nonetheless, the anointing still performs its spiritual function, providing strength to abandon false ways and to seek Christ with all one's heart.

---

6. OCIA 26 §§2, 54; RCIA 185 §§2, 22.

7. OCIA 206. The equivalent of OCIA 206 seems to be missing from the RCIA.

8. RCIA 33 §7; see OCIA 65 §7.

Minor Exorcisms

Major exorcisms are the ones that Hollywood has made famous. In actual practice they are performed only rarely in cases where the church fears the presence of demonic possession within a member of the baptized faithful.

More commonly, exorcisms take place in prebaptismal ceremonies. These do not imply demonic possession as much as demonic leverage in decision-making. Those who have not yet been baptized lack the grace that morally guides them throughout their lives. An exorcism that accompanies a scrutiny, for example, strengthens the elect against the sway of evil, anticipating the day of their baptism when they will formally renounce Satan.

During the catechumenate, the priest or deacon may offer minor exorcisms or blessings during Liturgies of the Word to strengthen the catechumens on their journey of faith (OCIA 108; RCIA 84). If he anoints with the oil of catechumens, he recites a minor exorcism just before (OCIA 130; RCIA 102).

The word "exorcism" consistently appears as a rubric or a heading in the ritual book. The formulas that the minister recites never have him pronounce the word aloud, partly because it is unnecessary, and probably because it would be easily misunderstood.

All exorcisms in the Catholic Church are now deprecatory, not imprecatory. That is, they address God, not the devil. Traditionally, they have concluded with an anointing, which gave this oil its earlier name, the oil of exorcism.

Anointing Children

The anointing of children complies with different procedures depending on the age of the child. One sequence pertains to an infant, another to a child of catechetical age enrolled in the catechumenate.

In the baptism of infants, the priest or deacon who conducts the ceremony prays an exorcism and then administers the oil of catechumens.[9] If he decides to omit the anointing, he lays a hand on the child instead (OBC 17, 151).

If an infant is to be baptized during the Easter Vigil, the prayer of exorcism and anointing take place earlier. The anointing of an infant with the oil of catechumens is always optional when the minister judges its omission necessary or desirable (OBC 24 §2), but in this case he may not anoint within the baptismal ceremony during the Easter Vigil. Instead, he may anoint the child sometime before the vigil, most likely on Holy Saturday itself but arguably even earlier (OBC 28 §1).

In the case of children of catechetical age who have been made catechumens, they receive their anointing after the rite of election, during the period of purification and enlightenment, when they are celebrating a scrutiny or penitential rite (OCIA 340; RCIA 301). This imitates a former tradition of administering the oil of exorcism at the scrutinies of adults.

A conference of bishops may elect to defer this anointing to the day of baptism. It then takes place between the renunciation of Satan and the confession of faith in the triune God (OCIA 354; RCIA 315). However, in the United States, as with adults, no children are to be anointed with the oil of catechumens on Holy Saturday or at the Easter Vigil.[10]

The Formula

As the priest or deacon anoints, he recites a simple formula: "May the strength of Christ the Savior protect you.

9. See OBC 49–50, for example.
10. RCIA 33 §7; see OCIA 65 §7.

As a sign of this we anoint you with the oil of salvation in the same Christ our Lord, who lives and reigns for ever and ever."[11]

The formula has two related parts. The first declares a prayer for strength. This immediately recalls the bishop's blessing over the oil of catechumens in the chrism Mass, where he addresses God with the title of "strength" and declares that oil is a sign of strength (OBO 22). In using the oil that the bishop blessed, the priest or deacon immediately prays that the strength of Christ will protect the one being anointed.

Christ is called "Savior." He is the one who saves from sin and from every power of evil. Because the oil still bears some connection with exorcisms, the minister calls upon Christ the supreme exorcist to support this anointing.

The minister prays that the strength of Christ will "protect" the one being anointed. The Latin word *muniat* can mean other things, including "strengthen," "secure," and "fortify." These meanings are subsumed into the English word "protect."

As ICEL worked on this translation, the commission agreed to turn the single Latin sentence into two. A literal translation would have begun something like this: "May the strength of Christ the Savior protect you, as a sign of which we anoint you. . ." But the meaning seemed less clear that way. For some years, ICEL favored the more literal translation at the request of the Vatican, but both parties now acknowledge that a looser translation at times leads to a better translation. In this case, ICEL itself perhaps felt the strength of Christ and made the final translation more understandable when spoken aloud.

---

11. OBC 50, for example.

Parts of the Body

Cyril of Jerusalem (+386) anointed catechumens from head to toe in the moments before their baptism. They stood naked, unashamed as Adam in paradise. He compared the anointing with olive oil to a grafting onto the olive tree that is Christ, the tree that Paul says received both wild and cultivated graftings (Rom 11:24); that is, both Gentile and Jewish believers who were coming to faith united themselves to Christ.[12] In a culture where adults took their baths in common, separated by gender, the baptism of naked catechumens was unsurprising.

Anointings today are more modest, though they do not exclude a generous application of oil. The priest or deacon anoints each catechumen on the breast, each hand, or other parts of the body (OCIA 130, 132; RCIA 102, 103). In the baptism of children, the "breast" is the only part of the body that the priest or deacon may anoint.[13]

ICEL strove for modesty in the translation of this rubric. The Latin word for "breast" is *pectus*, which can also mean "chest" or, more symbolically, "heart." In some English-speaking parts of the world, "chest" can mean the stomach, so the English translation avoids that word.

The "breast" proper is a highly sensual part of the body, especially of women; the liturgical word surely refers more narrowly to the area at the top of the sternum. The first provisional English translation of the post-Vatican II rites for the initiation of adults naively and somewhat scandalously translated the pertinent rubric this way: "Each catechumen

---

12. Edward Yarnold, SJ, *The Awe-Inspiring Rites of Initiation: The Origins of the R.C.I.A.*, 2nd ed. (Collegeville, MN: Liturgical Press, 1994), 76–77.

13. OBC 50, for example.

is anointed with the oil of catechumens on the breast or on both hands or even on other parts of the body, if this seems desirable."[14] The translation was changed to avoid the misinterpretation that it invited the minister to touch any parts of the catechumen's body that he found desirable.

In the case of infants, it would be hygienically unwise to anoint their hands, which children frequently place inside their mouths. The anointing of their breast is sometimes difficult if the parents have dressed the child in a garment that fastens tightly around the neck. They may need to loosen the garment in order for the minister to anoint. Anointing the top of the sternum suffices symbolically for what Cyril of Jerusalem practiced in the fourth century.

In the case of adults, the top of the sternum similarly is enough. However, the priest or deacon may anoint the hands. In practice, many catechumens feel most comfortable with this, as it involves a more public part of the body. It is difficult to know what other body parts would be fittingly anointed. The rubric's flexibility probably remains in honor of earlier historical practices.

The prayers associated with this ritual never allude to the potentially sensuous nature of the anointing. Although one can appreciate that the sacraments use elements that naturally bring delight, such as bread and wine, they aim to bring supernatural delight, an overcoming of bodily appetites. Especially in the case of the oil of catechumens, its purpose is to help the catechumens reorient their desires away from those of the flesh and toward those commanded by Christ.

---

14. *Rite of Christian Initiation of Adults*, Provisional Text (Washington, DC: United States Catholic Conference, 1974), 35.

Not Anointing with the Oil of Catechumens

The United States Conference of Catholic Bishops has approved the oil of catechumens but has not mandated it. Consequently, it remains one optional means of spiritual aid.

In the case of infants, the priest or deacon may omit the anointing if he judges it "pastorally necessary or desirable" (OBC 24:2). Either reason suffices.

The omission could be pastorally necessary if the minister has no oil. It could be pastorally desirable for a variety of reasons. The use of two oils may confuse the faithful without extensive catechesis on their purpose. In the baptism of infants, the use of this oil comes more from tradition than necessity. It may always be omitted, even for catechumens, and it is even more expendable in the case of children. Infants are not entering a catechumenate, and they will immediately be fortified with the waters of baptism, rendering the prebaptismal anointing less significant.

In the case of infants, if the anointing is omitted, the priest or deacon still places a hand on the child and says an adaptation of the prayer used during an anointing: "May the strength of Christ the Savior protect you; who lives and reigns for ever and ever."[15] This formula omits any reference to anointing, which the parallel formula names as a sign of the strength of Christ to protect. The minister still prays for the protection of Christ, but with handlaying rather than anointing.

If the anointing of adult catechumens is omitted, nothing replaces it. The catechumenate comes with a wide selection of prayers of exorcism and blessing that a priest or deacon may offer. Even these are optional, but they provide alternative

---

15. OBC 51, for example.

ways to help catechumens along their journey, whether or not they receive an anointing.

However, in two instances in the catechumenate, the anointing may be replaced with handlaying and the formula that appears in the baptism of children. In one case, the candidate either cannot go through all the steps of the full catechumenate, or the bishop judges the candidate so ready that initiation may proceed without delay (OCIA 240; RCIA 331). A candidate's inability to pass through the stages of the catechumenate could result from a shortage of time due to different factors: imminent military deployment, transfer from one prison to another, an impending move after graduation from a university, poor state of health, or a desire to celebrate initiation before an upcoming marriage, for example.

In such a situation, the priest may conduct a simpler order of adult initiation that compresses the various stages into one ceremony, much as the preconciliar rite of adult baptism had it. At this celebration, anointing with the oil of catechumens may follow a prayer of exorcism,[16] a pattern that the catechumenate otherwise retains only for the initiation of children of catechetical age, not for adults.[17] Here, though, because the adult is going to be baptized in the same ceremony, the conference of bishops may omit the oil of catechumens and replace it with the same text and gesture offered in the baptism of infants. In the United States, the oil is to be omitted whenever an adult is baptized.[18] The 1988 translation said it was "ordinarily" omitted at the baptism of

---

16. OCIA 255–56; RCIA 351–52.
17. OCIA 339–40; RCIA 300–301.
18. RCIA 33 §7; see OCIA 65 §7.

adults,[19] but the bishops seem to have intended that it always be omitted from that ceremony.

The second case when a priest may replace anointing with laying a hand on the catechumen concerns children of catechetical age. The children may be anointed at the scrutiny or penitential rite, or the conference of bishops may omit the anointing in favor of handlaying (OCIA 340; RCIA 301). The 1988 English translation allowed a priest in the United States to choose either form. If the children have already been anointed, for example, he may place a hand on each of them (RCIA 301). In that case, he uses the same prayer he says in the baptism of an infant when the anointing is omitted.

The omission of the anointing of catechumens may result from pastoral judgment or lack of oil. It is often replaced with another symbol and a similar prayer. Even when there is no anointing, the church likes to ensure that the catechumens or the infants receive strength for the journey of faith that lies ahead.

19. RCIA 352; see OCIA 256.

chapter three

Sacred Chrism

The Chrism Mass

Consecration

Chrism is the most important of the three oils. The liturgical texts refer to the oil of the sick and the oil of catechumens, but when they describe the third of the set, they generally include another adjective: "sacred" chrism. The bishop blesses the other two oils, and any priest may bless them in proper case of necessity. The bishop does not bless chrism; he consecrates it. No priest can do that.

The Catholic Church uses sacred chrism for sacraments that carry a character, meaning that a person may receive them only once: baptism, confirmation, and ordination. Additionally, when a new church and altar are dedicated, both the top of the altar and the walls the church are anointed with chrism, permanently assigning the building and the furnishing for sacred use.

Because chrism is a mixture of spices with oil, it possesses a pleasing aroma. The smell of chrism heightens one's awareness of its special nature. The nose alerts people that the effects of the anointing last beyond the moment. When administered during sacraments, the oil and the aroma sink into the skin and become one with the person anointed, the person who has imitated the one called Anointed: Christ.

Kingdom of Priests

The suggested entrance antiphon for the chrism Mass comes from the book of Revelation: "Jesus Christ has made us into a kingdom, priests for his God and Father. To him be glory and power for ever and ever. Amen."[1] It affirms the nature of the gathered assembly: a kingdom of priests made by Christ.

The suggested communion antiphon is the opening of Psalm 89, "I will sing for ever of your mercies, O Lord."[2] In a later verse of the same psalm, God speaks: "I have found my servant David, / and with my holy oil anointed him" (89:21, Abbey Psalms and Canticles). As David became king through an anointing, so the anointed community has become a kingdom of priests.

Many priests usually concelebrate the annual chrism Mass. The reference to priesthood in the entrance antiphon may lead people to conclude falsely that it refers to the ordained priests processing up the aisle. However, the antiphon celebrates the priesthood of the people. Through their baptism, Jesus Christ has made them a kingdom of priests, a designation symbolized by sacred chrism. The antiphon makes no attempt to encapsulate the application of all three oils; it focuses only on chrism. Nor does it summarize the many uses of chrism; it treats only initiation. The priests who concelebrate this Mass will administer its freshly consecrated chrism at their Easter Vigil.

The collect for the chrism Mass similarly focuses on the use of this sacred oil at baptism: "O God, who anointed your Only Begotten Son with the Holy Spirit and made him Christ and Lord, graciously grant that, being made sharers in his consecration, we may bear witness to your Redemption in the world" (7).

---

1. Roman Missal, The Chrism Mass 6; Rev 1:6.
2. Roman Missal, The Chrism Mass 13; Ps 89:2.

As the bishop prays the collect, he first recalls the baptism of Jesus, how God anointed him with the Holy Spirit, establishing him as Christ and Lord. Then he prays for all who have been baptized and anointed, for they share in the consecration of Christ. The baptized are to bear witness through the consecration they have received. They witness to the redemption that God works in the world.

Later in the Mass, as ministers carry the oils in procession, an echo of this collect resounds in the hymn, which calls upon Jesus Christ as the Redeemer. He is the Anointed One who fulfills the plan of God and to whom the baptized bear witness.

During the chrism Mass the priests renew their promises. Between that renewal and the number of priests concelebrating, one may wrongly conclude that the chrism Mass primarily concerns the anointing that happens during the ordination of priests. However, the liturgical texts uniformly spread the symbolism differently. They focus on the preparation of chrism for the upcoming baptisms. Throughout, the people are reminded that they have been anointed with this chrism and that they are called through their baptism to bear witness to the redemption.

Character

Saint Paul reminds the Ephesians that they were sealed for the day of redemption with the Holy Spirit of God (Eph 4:30). He tells the Corinthians that God has anointed them, put his seal on them, and placed the Spirit in their hearts. He numbers himself among those who received these benefits (2 Cor 1:21-22).

The Catholic tradition expresses this belief through its description of an indelible spiritual mark or character. Baptism so seals Christians with this mark that no sin can erase it (CCC 1272). The same seal consecrates them for worship and commits them to practice charity (1273). Because of this character, baptism cannot be repeated (1280).

Likewise, the sacrament of confirmation confers a character. Christ marks Christians with the seal of the Spirit so that they may bear witness (CCC 1304). A character is also imparted in the ordination of bishops and priests, by which bishops take the place of Christ himself and priests act in the person of Christ the head (1558, 1559, and 1563). In all these celebrations, a bishop anoints the candidate with sacred chrism.

Deacons also receive a character through their ordination, configuring them to Christ the deacon or servant of all (CCC 1570). However, theirs is the only sacramental celebration imparting a permanent character that does not include an anointing with chrism. Instead, their ministry of service particularizes the anointing they received at baptism.

The Code of Canon Law affirms this teaching: baptism, confirmation, and holy orders imprint a character.[3] The liturgy of the church expresses this belief through the use of sacred chrism. Once people are anointed with chrism for a particular purpose, they cannot be anointed with chrism again for the same purpose. The purpose is permanent.

Mixing Chrism

Chrism must be mixed before it can be consecrated. This usually happens during the chrism Mass. As ministers carry three large containers of oil to the sanctuary, they also carry a separate container of perfume, such as balsam. Then, after the bishop has blessed the oils of the sick and of catechumens, he pours the aromas into the third container of oil and stirs them together (OBO 23). This may take place either after

---

3. Canon 845 §1.

the procession of the gifts or after communion, but always immediately after the blessing of the oil of catechumens.

The rubric notes that the bishop mixes the oil in silence. Prior to the revisions of the liturgy, the bishop offered prayers of exorcism and blessing over the balsam.[4] The simplification of this ritual after Vatican II fit with the simplification of others, such as the preparation of incense and of baptismal water. In the past, some elements of the liturgy presumed that objects of the created world needed exorcism before they could be put to sacred use. Such a preliminary treatment of balsam has been removed from the chrism Mass in favor of recognizing the goodness of creation and the potency of the prayer of consecration.

The mixing, therefore, happens in silence. Often the participants can hear the splash of one liquid poured into the other and the ring of the bishop's twirling metal spoon striking the insides of the container. These unusual sounds intensify the unique sacredness of the upcoming consecration.

However, the liturgy permits the mixture to be stirred before the chrism Mass begins. The liquids may be combined in the sacristy (OBO 5, 23). If this happens, the rubric does not limit the action to the bishop. Presumably, a sacristan or deacon could mix the oils, in the way that a deacon may add water to wine before the priest praises God for the mingling in the chalice during the preparation of the gifts at any Mass.

The rubrics do not explain what would make this advance preparation desirable. Perhaps a preliminary preparation would shorten the duration of the Mass. Perhaps the mixing is less essential than the consecration, and removing it to the sacristy keeps the community's focus on the consecration,

---

4. See Paul Turner, *Glory in the Cross: Holy Week in the Third Edition of* The Roman Missal (Collegeville, MN: Liturgical Press, 2011), 51.

the proper highlight of the ceremony. Perhaps some would find the mixing too redolent of pagan practices observed in their culture. The rubrics do not say. Most commonly, people find the mixing of the chrism an appealing ceremony to witness, highlighting the special nature of this oil, which the bishop is about to consecrate.

If the mixing takes place during the liturgy, the sacristan prepares for it. A vessel of the fragrances is set in the sacristy or another suitable place, ready for its procession with the oils. A table is situated in the sanctuary in such a way that the people may see the actions and participate in the ceremony. If the bishop cannot preside over this part of the Mass from his cathedra because of its distance from the table, the sacristan makes ready the bishop's faldstool, a chair that is portable yet sufficiently dignified (OBO 13).

If the mixing of chrism is carried out in private, its deemphasis helps the prayer of consecration gather the attention of the faithful. If it is carried out in public, the bishop's attentive preparation anticipates the sacredness of the prayer he is about to say.

Introducing the Consecration

Of the three prayers over the oils, only the consecration of chrism comes with a special introduction. The people always pray silently along with the bishop, answering "Amen" to the conclusion of each prayer. But even before beginning the prayer of consecration, the bishop verbally enlists the assistance of the assembled faithful. He asks everyone to pray that God will "bless and sanctify this oil, so that all who are outwardly anointed with it may be inwardly transformed" (OBO 24).

The English translation for this introduction is comprehensible, but the Latin original sustains nuances. For example, the English hopes that those who are "outwardly anointed" may be "inwardly transformed." In Latin, both verbs refer to an anointing: *peruncti* and *liniantur*. It means more that those who are anointed on the outside may be thereby anointed inside as well.

The introduction concludes with the hope that the anointed will share in "eternal salvation," whereas the Latin has *divinæ redemptionis* or "divine redemption." The word "redemption" appears here as it does in the collect and in the hymn for the procession of the oils. It shows the mission of the Anointed One, Christ, who came as the Redeemer.

The bishop is about to offer the most solemn of the three prayers unique to this Mass. He asks for assistance. He appeals to the assembled community of Christians, the anointed ones.

Breathing

The bishop may breathe upon the mixture (OBO 25 §1). This action was formerly obligatory; now it is done "if appropriate." He used to make the sign of the cross with his breath, moving his head in the process. The rubrics no longer indicate that action, but some bishops continue the practice.

The rubrics do not explain the breathing, but it seems to represent a kind of epiclesis. The bishop himself has received gifts of the Holy Spirit for his ministry, and he confers gifts of the Spirit whenever he confirms. The breath from his mouth evokes Jesus' conversation with Nicodemus, in which he compares the blowing of the wind with the action of the Holy Spirit (John 3:8).

The symbol may be lost on people who only associate breaths with the extinguishing of altar candles at church or of birthday candles at home. If so, or for any other reason, the bishop may omit this part of the ritual. He uses more familiar gestures when he recites the words of consecrating chrism: he extends his hands in prayer, and he makes the sign of the cross with one hand in blessing.

Author, Beginning

The ritual book offers the bishop a choice between two prayers that consecrate chrism. The first is a reworking of the traditional prayer that has been part of the chrism Mass since at least the seventh century. The second was newly composed after Vatican II.

Both prayers address God under the unusual title, "author," the cognate of the Latin word *auctor*. The word "Creator" also works as a translation, but the Latin word implies something more. God creates like an artist. In its opening words the Nicene Creed professes belief in God, the "maker" of heaven and earth. This translates the original Greek word from this line of the Creed, ποιητής, from which English gets its word "poet." The church believes in God, the Poet of heaven and earth. The word "author" implies more than bringing into being. It implies creating beauty.

In this case, the bishop acknowledges God as "the author of all growth and spiritual progress" (OBO 25 §1). God's creating activity continues through the physical and spiritual growth of all things made. In a few words, the bishop already establishes the themes of praising God for the creation of natural oil and for spiritual refreshment, which that oil achieves when set aside for sacred purposes.

Naturally, the prayer turns to the creation of the world, storied in the opening pages of the Bible. In particular, the bishop mentions the creation of fruit-bearing trees. According to Genesis, God created them on the third day (1:11). The bishop draws a direct line from the first chapter of the Bible to the present moment. God commanded the earth to bring forth trees, of which arose olive trees, "providers of this most rich oil, so that their fruit might serve for sacred

Chrism" (OBO 25 §1). He suggests that God had chrism in mind from the third day of creation.

Spirit of Prophecy

The prayer meditates on passages from the Old Testament that prophesy the function of chrism in the contemporary church. This section opens with two images, presented in reverse chronological order: King David and the dove of Noah's ark.

David appears here not so much as king but as songwriter. The prayer acknowledges the tradition that David himself composed the book of Psalms. Although biblical scholarship concludes that many writers over some centuries composed the songs of the psalter, this older tradition personalizes the spirit of prophecy that Christians perceive in the book.

Specifically, the bishop recalls a line from Psalm 104, which praises God for the gift of grass and plants, bread and wine, and then "oil, to make faces shine" (v. 15). As the prayer of consecration puts it, David "sang of the oil that would gladden our faces." The bishop refers to the oil he is consecrating as the source that "causes our faces to be joyful and serene" (OBO 25 §1).

As Noah, his family, and the animals waited for the flood-waters to subside sufficiently for disembarkation, he released a dove for signs of landfall. Eventually the bird returned with the long-awaited sign of new life in its beak: a leaf from an olive tree (Gen 8:11). The flood had wiped away all the world's beings, including humans with their offenses (Gen 7:21). For Christians, the flood became a sign of the waters of baptism, which wipe away all sin, and the olive branch, a foreshadowing of the oil of initiation.

These two biblical events—the composing of the psalms and the receding of the flood—provide the bishop's prayer of consecration prophetic images for confirmation and baptism.

Perhaps they appear in reverse chronological order to bestow their proper relevance to the prayer at hand: The bishop is not blessing water for baptism; he is consecrating chrism for initiation and other purposes. The prophecy pertaining to oil alone precedes a second one that includes water.

The Priesthood of Aaron

The sequence of prophetic images from the Old Testament proceeds to the anointing of Aaron. God commanded Moses to anoint Aaron and his sons, consecrating them as priests (Exod 30:30). In the elaborate ceremony that followed, Moses washed the men with water (Lev 8:6) and then sprinkled them with a mixture of oil and sacrificial blood (Lev 8:30).

The bishop's prayer recalls these events: "You also commanded your servant Moses to make his brother Aaron a priest, by pouring this oil upon him after he had been washed in water" (OBO 25 §1). The prayer seems to move from the Old Testament antecedents for the use of chrism in initiation rites to the passages that foreshadow the use of chrism in the ordination of priests. However, the liturgical texts of the chrism Mass focus on initiation from start to finish. In this case, because the anointing of Aaron links to the passage of his washing, the prayer points again to a particular contemporary use of chrism: not to the ordained priesthood, but to the common priesthood of the faithful signified in the postbaptismal anointing with chrism.

This focus on the priesthood of the people, faithful to the long history of this prayer, certainly appealed to the revisers of the liturgy after Vatican II. The priesthood of the people undergirds their full, conscious, active participation in the liturgy. The prayer for the consecration of chrism already anticipates this right and duty of the baptized and anointed people of God.

The Baptism of Jesus

The bishop finally recalls the baptism of Jesus, the pivotal moment that swings the prophecies of old into the new dispensation. Most unusually, all four gospels and the Acts of the Apostles all bear witness to this event.[5] As Jesus was washed in the Jordan, the Father sent the Holy Spirit in the likeness of a dove. The bishop addresses the Father: in this event "you were seen to confirm clearly what the prophet David had foretold in song, that Christ would be anointed with the oil of gladness above his companions" (OBO 25 §1).

All the biblical testimony confirms the appearance of the Holy Spirit. None of the testimony pretends to declare that John the Baptist literally anointed Jesus with oil. However, in Acts of the Apostles, Peter catechized the household of Cornelius that in this baptism, God anointed Jesus with the Holy Spirit and power.[6] Peter used the image of anointing to show how, at the baptism of Jesus, the Father had set him apart for his ministry through the gift of the Holy Spirit.

Here again, the connection between the washing of Christ in water and the conferral of the Holy Spirit through a spiritual anointing shows that the bishop is praying about the administration of this chrism in the rites of initiation. Just as Jesus was declared God's Son and anointed with the Spirit at his baptism, so catechumens will become adopted children of God, anointed with the Spirit, at their forthcoming rites of initiation.

King David returns at the end of this first major section of the prayer with one more prophecy. The bishop alludes to Psalm 45, a song probably composed for a royal wedding. God, the king's own God, has anointed him "with the oil of

5. Matt 3:16; Mark 1:10; Luke 3:22; John 1:32; and Acts 10:38.
6. Acts 10:38; see also Acts 4:27.

gladness above other kings," making even his robes fragrant with spices (45:8). The Roman Gradual and the Simple Gradual recommend the same psalm be sung at communion of the chrism Mass. In the Bible, the letter to the Hebrews applies this psalm to God's Son (Heb 1:9). At his baptism, Christ was metaphorically anointed with this oil of gladness. He thus began his ministry to woo his bride, the church.

At the beginning of his public ministry, Jesus entered a synagogue in Nazareth and read from the scroll of the prophet Isaiah, applying the message to himself. He cites a passage with the same metaphor found in Psalm 45: The Spirit of the Lord anointed him to bring good news to the afflicted. In the full passage from Isaiah, the anointed one in turn gives to those who mourn an oil of gladness.[7]

As the newly baptized receive their anointing with fragrant chrism, they too accept a mission. God anoints them with the best of oil. They become glad of heart. They enter the world as on their wedding day, rejoicing in a partnership with Christ.

Concelebrants' Extension of Hands

The concelebrants extend their right hands toward the chrism for the remainder of the bishop's prayer (OBO 25 §1). The lengthy prayer of consecration falls into two main divisions, as do many liturgical prayers. First it acknowledges the great deeds of God, and then it makes its petition. Even the Lord's Prayer first praises God's holy name before praying for the coming of the kingdom, daily bread, and forgiveness. Before making a request, the bishop has praised God for the Old Testament figures who foreshadowed the use of oils in the Christian rites of initiation, which participate in

---

7. Isa 61:1-3; see Luke 4:18.

elements of Jesus' own baptism: washing with water and anointing with the Spirit. As the bishop reaches the transitional moment of the prayer, the concelebrants join him—not in words but in gesture.

The participation of concelebrants in this way began after Vatican II. Concelebration on this occasion has a long history, and the practice expanded to other events after the council. Concelebrants are even offered a gesture at the consecration of the bread and wine: They may extend their right hands if this seems appropriate.[8] In practice, most priests do, even though the gesture is optional. It gives concelebrants a visible way to participate in the consecration of the bread and wine during any eucharistic prayer.

In a similar way, in another prayer of consecration, this time over chrism, the priests extend their right hands. In this case the gesture is not optional; all the concelebrants make it together.

The bishop is about to pray that God will pour into the oil "the strength of the Holy Spirit" (OBO 25 §1). This prayer is a kind of epiclesis, then, similar to the section of the eucharistic prayers that calls upon the Father to send the Holy Spirit upon the bread and wine. In the eucharistic prayer, concelebrants extend both hands toward the offerings during the epiclesis, palms down, and they may then extend their right hands toward the offerings during the consecration. The same gesture links the consecration of chrism with the consecration of bread and wine. In fact, the gesture sheds light on the consecration of the bread and wine: Even though the concelebrants have already extended both their hands for the epiclesis, when they extend only their right hands at

---

8. Roman Missal, The General Instruction of the Roman Missal [GIRM] 222c, 227c, 230c, 233c.

the time of the consecration, they repeat the gesture that the prayer of consecration of chrism associates with an epiclesis. In this light, the concelebrants' gesture during the consecration appears less indicative; that is, it does not merely point to the bread and wine. It appears more epicletic, continuing the prayer for the coming of the Holy Spirit upon these elements. The rubrics of the Mass do not tell a priest how to hold his right hand, but the evidence from the chrism Mass suggests that in both instances the priests will express the intention of the prayer better if their right palms are down—indicating not the elements but the direction for the outpouring of the Holy Spirit.

The concelebrants say nothing. The prayer belongs to the bishop. But they are present as his "witnesses and co-workers in the ministry of the sacred Chrism" (OBO 14). They extend their hands only in the consecration of chrism, not for the blessing of the other oils. They unite with the bishop to pray for consecration and administer chrism, especially at baptisms and the occasions when they confirm. Priests can do none of that without the Holy Spirit, the bishop, and sacred chrism.

Sign of the Cross

As the bishop sanctifies the oil of chrism, he makes the sign of the cross over it, traditionally with his right hand. Ordained ministers frequently use this sign to indicate blessing. At Mass, a priest blesses the offerings during the eucharistic prayer. He also blesses the people at the conclusion of the service. Throughout the Book of Blessings, deacons as well as priests use the sign of the cross to bless objects and people.

Each such gesture evokes the cross of Christ, the instrument of salvation. It implies the grace of the resurrection through and beyond the pathway of death. Each sign of the cross identifies the object or person blessed with the ministry of Christ, his acceptance of mortality, and his promise of redemption.

Immediately after making this gesture and praying for the Holy Spirit, the bishop declares that chrism receives its name from Christ. In a way, this sounds backwards. "Christ" means "Anointed One," so Jesus received his title from one common use of oil. However, as the Messiah, the Christ, the Anointed One, Jesus bestows his own title back upon this special oil appointed for sacred purposes in the church. Chrism is consecrated by the outpouring of the Holy Spirit, and it represents the continuing ministry of Jesus Christ.

As the bishop sanctifies the chrism, he places it into the hands of the Father, imploring the outpouring of the Holy Spirit, whose coming Jesus promised at his passion. The bishop places the administration of this chrism, especially upon the newly baptized, under the sign of the cross of Christ.

Martyrs

The bishop notes that God has anointed with chrism his "priests, prophets, kings, and martyrs" (OBO 25 §1). The list is curious because of the addition of martyrs.

At first, this appears to be another reference to the Old Testament passages about the anointing of certain important leaders within the community. However, the bishop explicitly says that these people have been anointed with chrism, not with some other prophetic oil.

This removes the possibility that he means a metaphorical anointing. In English it is sometimes said of a person that he or she is the anointed successor of someone else. This expression does not mean the reception of a physical anointing, but a general agreement that a person is owed a certain position. Sometimes the person so referenced has not earned the position or even demonstrated sufficient readiness for it. In spite of these conditions, and perhaps because of them, the successor is not called "elected," "practiced," or "expert," but "anointed." Common agreement constitutes spiritual anointing. That does not apply here, where the bishop lists those whom God anointed with chrism.

The clue to the bishop's meaning hides in the surprising addition of martyrs to the list. Most commonly in Christian circles, the baptismal anointing with chrism pertains to a share in the ministries of priest, prophet, and king. The English translation of the bishop's prayer of consecration keeps those ministries in that order, as they appear for example in the minister's proclamation when he anoints a newly baptized infant: "[God the Father] now anoints you with the Chrism of salvation, so that you may remain members of Christ, Priest, Prophet, and King, unto eternal life" (OBC 62). The bishop's prayer for the consecration of chrism adds the final category, martyrs.

However, in the original Latin of this prayer of consecration, the bishop names these ministries in a different order: *sacerdotes, reges, prophetas, et martyres tuos*: "your priests, kings, prophets, and martyrs." Martyrs are equated with prophets, and because of their exalted status within the hierarchy of saints, martyrs come last in the list, drawing prophets to a position after the kings in their wake. The connection between prophets and martyrs comes from the book of Revelation. Observing the carnage in Babylon, the seer hears a voice that laments, amid other woes, the ruination of the great city, the disappearance of its music and sources of light, and, importantly, the discovery of the blood of prophets and saints (Rev 18:24). Jesus himself recalled the slaughtering of prophets from Abel to Zechariah.[9] In the new covenant, some Christians—the anointed followers of Christ, those who have served as prophets—have suffered as martyrs.

---

9. Luke 11:49-51; Matt 23:34-35.

The bishop's prayer of consecration lists those baptized and anointed with chrism. They are members of a priestly people. They lead by example with Christ the King. They prophesy, bringing his Word into the world. Prophets take risks, and some became martyrs for the faith. Disciples have done all this in the name of Christ, who gave his title to the sacred oil of chrism.

Confirming the Chrism

The bishop asks the Father to "confirm the Chrism" he created. This request advances the second main division of the prayer of consecration in which the bishop makes his grand petition to God. By confirming the chrism, God will make it "a sacred sign of perfect salvation and life" for the newly baptized (OBO 25 §1).

In asking the Father to confirm, the bishop uses the same verb that returns when he applies chrism in the sacrament of confirmation. By calling the chrism a sign of "perfect" salvation and life, he uses another word associated with the same sacrament. The Catechism says that confirmation is "the completion of baptismal grace" (CCC 1285). Confirmation polishes baptism, seals the candidate with the Spirit, and continues the initiation ceremonies that prepare the Christian to bear witness in the world.

In context, though, the word "confirm" probably means nothing more than "strengthen" or "appoint." It shows the designated purpose of chrism. Favorably, the verb resonates with one of its key applications among the sacraments of initiation.

This petition begins a section of the bishop's lengthy prayer that shows how ICEL's translators strove for comprehension. In Latin, the entire second half, the part during which the concelebrants raise their hands toward the chrism, is all one sentence—over one hundred words long. It has a certain majesty to it in the original. By comparison, the first sentence of the United States Declaration of Independence is over eighty words long. It shows a sense of well-reasoned purpose. However, in spoken English and in contemporary culture, a lengthy, grammatically complex sentence sounds more prolix than inspirational. Remembering the people's difficulties in comprehending such parts of their recent translation of the Roman Missal, the bishops on the commission broke up this one long sentence into five shorter ones.

The main verb for all of these petitions appears only in the first of these sentences. It accompanies the moment when the bishop makes the sign of the cross over the chrism. He asks God to "sanctify" the oil.

In this case, when the bishop prays that God will "confirm the Chrism," he is not really making a new request. He expresses one way that the sanctification of the chrism will have its effect. He prays that God will sanctify it so that he may confirm it as a sacred sign.

Holy Temple

Saint Paul told the Corinthians that their body is the temple of the Holy Spirit (1 Cor 6:19). The Spirit dwells there. Their bodies are not their own. In a subsequent letter, he told the same audience that he and they were the aroma of Christ to God (2 Cor 2:15). They were like a sacrificial offering alighting a pleasing fragrance.

These passages probably lie behind the next section of the prayer of consecration. The bishop asks that "those formed into a temple" of divine majesty may "be made fragrant with the innocence of a life" pleasing to God (OBO 25 §1).

In this dense sentence, the bishop makes several affirmations. In chronological order, baptism achieved "the cleansing of the stain of their first birth." This alludes to baptism's purifying power over original sin. The bishop also implies that confirmation is responsible for the "holiness infused through this anointing" (OBO 25 §1). These sacraments result in making Christians temples of God's majesty, as Saint Paul had declared. The bishop prays that those thus formed into such a temple may lead innocent lives that please God as does fragrance.

ICEL's translators struggled to get this right. They considered using "corruption" instead of "stain," but that sounded as if giving birth were somehow a corrupt activity. They considered "original sin" for "first birth," but that appeared overly catechetical. They strove to preserve a poetic imagery that taught the effects of baptism, while avoiding misconceptions.

The density of this sentence results from the order of the elements that bury baptism in the middle. It moves from temple to anointing to cleansing to fragrance—not the chronology in which the sacraments are celebrated. However, the words probably pile up this way because the prayer concerns chrism, so the petition mentions its properties before it speaks of the power of baptism. Even though the sentence is fairly short, its arrangement complicates its interpretation.

As with the previous section, this petition depends on the main verb "sanctify." The bishop is not so much asking a new intention as he is detailing the results of what happens from his primary request that God sanctify the chrism. One fruit is the formation of those who are anointed into a temple of God's majesty.

Incorruptible Garment
Saint Paul also wrote to the Corinthians that their perishable and mortal body should put on imperishability and immortality. This will give Christians their victory over death in Christ (1 Cor 15:53-55).

The bishop alludes to this in the next section of the prayer of consecration. He prays that those who are anointed with the chrism may "be clothed with the garment of an incorruptible gift" (OBO 25 §1).

Oil is itself a kind of garment, worn directly on the flesh. As this section of the prayer also affirms, chrism confers "royal, priestly, and prophetic dignity." This is the "incorruptible gift" that the bishop metaphorically calls a garment (OBO 25 §1). Through the anointing with chrism, Christians put on that gift, that dignity, which will give them victory over death.

As with the previous sentences, this one further explains the main petition, "sanctify." If God sanctifies the oil, then those anointed with it will be clothed in his incorruptible gift as they receive the divinely instituted sacrament of confirmation. In a way, the bishop need not pray that those anointed with chrism be clothed in this garment. That is the inevitable result if God would simply sanctify the oil.

Life and Glory

To conclude the consecration prayer, the bishop asks that those anointed with chrism be thus made "partakers of eternal life and sharers of heavenly glory." The immediate effects of chrism sanctify the people for their lives as Christians. Its ultimate effect guides them toward eternal life.

This section of the prayer returns to the sacraments of initiation. It prays "for those born again of water and the Holy Spirit," that this oil may be for them "the Chrism of salvation" (OBO 25 §1). Baptism begins their life as a Christian, which has its ultimate purpose in life after death.

The bishop describes the baptized as those who experience what Jesus taught Nicodemus: No one enters the kingdom of God without being born of water and the Spirit (John 3:5).

By calling chrism an oil "of salvation," the bishop recalls the title of Christ sung in the procession of the oils: Redeemer. As Christ is the redeemer of the human race, so this chrism signifies his ultimate desire to save his people.

This final sentence of the prayer is the last section that falls under the main verb, "sanctify." The bishop lists one more result of the sanctification of the oil. If God makes it holy, it will become the chrism of salvation with the power of making those anointed with it partakers of life and glory. The sentence links baptism and the anointing with chrism, as if the two are indistinguishable. The prayer has its deepest meaning for those who will be confirmed at their baptismal ceremony during the Easter Vigil in the days following the chrism Mass.

This draws to a close the first alternative of the prayers that consecrate chrism. This one, steeped in the imagery of the Old Testament, shows the fruitfulness of the anointing in the new covenant. It is the older of the two, but the bishop may choose the other.

Author of the Sacraments

Like the first, the second option for the bishop's prayer of consecration of chrism calls God "author." Whereas the first called God the author of all natural and spiritual growth, the second calls God the "author of the Sacraments and bestower of life" (OBO 25 §2). While the first prayer began with an excursus on oil in the economy of salvation, this one turns more to anointing in the sacraments of the church.

The main verbal phrase, "we give thanks," immediately distinguishes the structure of this prayer. It resembles a eucharistic prayer, which declares with the first person plural that the community offers thanks to God. The first prayer of consecrating chrism keeps the main verb in the second person, directly addressing God. In this version, the bishop wants God to read clearly the hearts of the people who are giving thanks.

Whereas the first prayer enumerates examples of anointings in the Old Testament, this prayer gathers them into a generic affirmation: "in the ancient covenant you foreshadowed the mystery of sanctifying oil" (OBO 25 §2). As the first prayer guides these prototypes toward the baptism of Christ, so this prayer says that the mystery of oil shines forth uniquely in God's "beloved Son." At his baptism, Jesus was anointed with the Holy Spirit as the voice of God bestowed that title upon him.

These are examples of God's "ineffable" goodness. ICEL left in place this adjective that had provoked some controversy in translating the Roman Missal. A Latin equivalent of the word "ineffable" appears in the missal nearly fifty times, but it became a touchpoint for those who criticized the revision for using a vocabulary beyond ordinary speech. The missal's translators replaced it with other English words, such as "wondrous." In this case, given the unique nature of the chrism Mass and that only a bishop pronounces this prayer, "ineffable" remains. Fittingly, it is a word that means a quality for which words fail.

Holy Spirit and Paschal Mystery

The bishop calls the death and resurrection of Christ "the Paschal Mystery," a phrase much loved by Vatican II, as it helped Catholics look beyond the sorrow of the cross of Christ to the fullness of Easter joy. He then recalls the first sending of the Holy Spirit into the world at Pentecost.

Each Pentecost Sunday, when offering the preface at Mass, the priest declares before God, "bringing your Paschal Mystery to completion, you bestowed the Holy Spirit today on those you made your adopted children." In a similar way, this prayer of consecrating chrism stitches the role of the Holy Spirit onto the mission of Christ: "when your Son, our Lord, had saved the human race through the Paschal Mystery, he filled your Church with the Holy Spirit" (OBO 25 §2). The sending of the Holy Spirit on the first Pentecost completed the mission of the Son.

The bishop notes that the entire church accepts this mission from the Spirit. The church receives the gifts of the Holy Spirit so that salvation "might be brought to completion." The prayer alludes to the effect of the sacrament of confirmation, when those who have already participated in the death and resurrection of Christ by their baptism receive the grace of the Spirit through anointing with chrism. This interior completion of the paschal mystery equips them to bear witness to Christ.

Postbaptismal Anointing

The bishop proclaims the power of the anointings in baptism and confirmation. As with other liturgical prayers, the first part gives thanks for God's wondrous deeds. The other prayer for consecrating chrism explored biblical testimony, and this second option proclaims the gifts that flow from the sacraments. The bishop has already called God the "author of the Sacraments." In this section of the prayer, he explicitly describes the initiation sacraments.

For confirmation, the bishop mentions those "strengthened by the anointing of the Spirit" and "conformed" to Christ (OBO 25 §2). The Catechism lists these among the purposes of confirmation: It unites one more firmly to Christ, and it gives a special strength of the Holy Spirit (CCC 1303).The bishop says that the gift of confirmation is bestowed on those "born again in the cleansing waters of Baptism," as Jesus explained this mystery to Nicodemus (John 3:7). The postbaptismal anointing with chrism, administered by a priest, associates the newly baptized with the "prophetic, priestly and kingly office" of Christ (OBO 25 §2). By mentioning these functions together with the fruits of the gifts of the Holy Spirit, the bishop includes both baptism and confirmation in his reasons for giving thanks to God. He thus draws the first part of the prayer of consecration to a fitting close.

Concelebrants' Extension of Hands and Sign of the Cross

As in the first option, the concelebrants extend their right hands toward the chrism when this prayer reaches its point of transition (OBO 25 §2). The bishop is about to make his petition. Up to now he has expressed the many reasons for giving God thanks for the gift of chrism and the continued outpouring of the gifts of the Holy Spirit upon the church. Having gained God's attention with fitting praise, he calls upon God's goodness to provide more chrism so that the church may continue its divine mission.

The bishop makes the sign of the cross over the mixed oil, as he does in the first alternative of this prayer. By this action, which he performs as the concelebrants extend their hands, the bishop demonstrates his primary role as the priests express their association with his ministry, especially when they anoint with chrism.

The bishop uses a descriptive term for the chrism: "this mingling of fragrance and oil" (OBO 25 §2). The word "chrism" appears nowhere in the second version of the prayer of consecration because that is what results from the prayer. At the moment of blessing, the bishop does not presume that the mixture is already chrism. He simply describes the contents of the vessel. ICEL had some discussion about the proper translation of the word for these contents. Some wanted "mixture." "Blend" was also proposed, but it reminded some translators of the process for making whiskey. The word "mingling" best seemed to express the contents and the action that produce the substance for what will become sacred chrism.

The bishop asks God that "this mingling of fragrance and oil may become for us a sacrament of your blessing" (OBO 25 §2). He therefore asks for the blessing more obliquely than in the first alternative. He asks not so much for a blessing of the oil but that the use of the oil may convey God's blessing.

This calls to mind other examples of alternative prayers of blessing. On the feast of the Presentation of the Lord, for example, the priest has two choices for the blessing that precedes the opening procession. He may bless the candles in the first option, or with the second option he may ask God to pour light into the hearts of the faithful who carry the candles.[10] On Ash Wednesday the priest also has two choices. In the second option he blesses the ashes, but in the first he blesses the people to be marked with the ashes. On Palm Sunday he likewise has two choices. In the first he asks God to sanctify the branches, and in the second he prays for an increase in faith of those who hold the branches (6).

In this second option of the prayer that consecrates chrism, as the bishop implores God concerning the future uses of the oil, he makes the sign of the cross with his hand, the traditional gesture for invoking upon persons and objects the blessing of God.

The Effects of Chrism
Finally, the bishop summarizes the effects of chrism in its various usages. In anticipation he prays that those who will be confirmed may receive "in abundance the gifts of the Holy Spirit." Thinking ahead to the dedication of churches and altars, the bishop prays that the chrism may "adorn with the splendor of holiness the places and things signed by sacred oils."

He then asks God "above all" that this chrism may "bring to completion the growth of your Church." This is accomplished

---

10. Roman Missal, February 2, Presentation of the Lord 5.

primarily through baptism. When baptizing an infant, the priest or deacon anoints with the oil of chrism. In this way, chrism complements the increase of members of the church.

However, the bishop acknowledges in the prayer's closing words that the goal of baptism is not simply to get new members but to reach the summits of God's own plan. The church will continue evangelizing and baptizing "until she reaches that measure of fullness in which you, resplendent with eternal light, will be all in all with Christ in the Holy Spirit, for ever and ever" (OBO 25 §2).

Several scriptural passages lie behind this petition. The bishop calls God the one who is resplendent with eternal light because the book of Psalms praises God with the declaration, "Resplendent are you" (76:5).

The bishop anticipates that the spread of baptism will reach the measure of fullness because Paul wrote to the Ephesians that he looks for the day when "all of us come to the unity of the faith and of the knowledge of the Son of God, to maturity, to the measure of the full stature of Christ" (Eph 4:13).

The bishop envisions that at the end of time these sacraments will reach their ultimate purpose, as Paul wrote to the Corinthians, "When all things are subjected to him, then the Son himself will also be subjected to the one who put all things in subjection under him, so that God may be all in all" (1 Cor 15:28).

In this way, the second option for the prayer of consecration reflects on the sacraments of the church, gifts from God, put into usage through solemn ceremonies, producing an effect on the individuals who receive them and anticipating their day of completion, a day when the church will need no sacramental signs because God has become all in all.

The Baptism of Children

Baptismal Anointing

Among the effects of baptism, "human beings are incorporated into the church and are built up together into a dwelling place of God in the Spirit and into a royal priesthood and a holy nation." When the baptized are anointed with chrism, the liturgy makes clear that unchangeable effect.[11]

Both the Order of Baptism of Children and the Rite of Christian Initiation of Adults share a general introduction pertaining to Christian initiation. The group working on these revisions after Vatican II crafted one introduction that would serve both rituals, perhaps envisioning that it would all appear in a single volume. A similar general introduction heads the rites of ordination of a bishop, priest and deacon, which do appear in one book.

At times, the general introduction for Christian initiation struggles to cover both circumstances of baptism, and the use of chrism provides one example. When a priest baptizes an adult, he administers confirmation immediately. But when a priest or deacon baptizes an infant, he administers a different postbaptismal anointing with chrism. The introduction to the Order of Baptism of Children clarifies the meaning of this anointing, which signifies "the royal priesthood of the baptized and enrollment into the company of the People of God" (OBC 18 §3).

The roots of this twofold anointing with chrism probably lie with the *Apostolic Tradition*, a third- or fourth-century church order that served as foundational material for the post-Vatican II revisions to the catechumenate, ordination ceremonies, and even the composition of Eucharistic Prayer

---

11. OBC, Christian Initiation, General Introduction 4.

II. Believed to have at least some of its origins in Rome, this document influenced the faithful development of liturgical rituals after the council.

In the case of initiation, the *Apostolic Tradition* tells of two anointings with chrism: one administered by a priest, and the other by the bishop.[12] The priest anointed at the baptismal font in the name of Jesus Christ, and the bishop, praying for the gift of the Holy Spirit, laid hands on the newly baptized and anointed them inside the church.

The Catholic Church still retains two alternative initiatory anointings, one in infant baptism, the other—confirmation— for adult baptism; one administered by a priest or deacon, the other by the priest who baptizes; one on the crown of the head, the other on the forehead; one accompanied by a prayer pertaining to Christ, and the other with one pertaining to the Holy Spirit. Both use the same oil, but different words with different purposes.

When the general introduction for Christian initiation names among the effects of baptism a sharing in a royal priesthood by means of an anointing, it means the anointing of an infant. The introduction relies on two passages from New Testament letters. Saint Paul told the Ephesians that they "are built together spiritually into a dwelling place for God" (Eph 2:22), and Saint Peter wrote to the newly baptized, "you are a chosen race, a royal priesthood, a holy nation, God's own people" (1 Pet 2:9).

This latter passage especially evokes the purpose of anointing with chrism. As kings received an anointing, so does each baptized member of the community. All of them have royal

12. Paul F. Bradshaw, Maxwell E. Johnson, and L. Edward Phillips, *The Apostolic Tradition: A Commentary* (Minneapolis: Augsburg Fortress, 2002), 118–19.

dignity as well as royal responsibilities. The lectionary recommends this passage for proclamation on occasions such as Christian initiation, the anniversary of the dedication of a church, and the Mass for the Laity. The Book of Blessings recommends it for blessing a parish hall or catechetical center, a new building site, and the departure of pilgrims. It has dozens of other usages, including an inspiration for certain intercessions in the Liturgy of the Hours.[13]

The Rite of Christian Initiation of Adults, after the general introduction it shares with the Order of Baptism of Children, has its own introduction, which also describes the postbaptismal anointing among various ceremonies such as the white garment and the burning candle. This introduction similarly declares that the anointing with chrism after baptism signifies royal priesthood and the enrollment of the baptized into the people of God (OCIA 33; RCIA 214). However, this anointing is generally reserved for infants.

Newly baptized adults receive this postbaptismal anointing only if for some reason their confirmation is separated from their baptism (OCIA 224; RCIA 228). Only a serious reason should cause this separation because of the ancient practice that kept the two sacraments together (OCIA 35; RCIA 216). The rubrics do not explain what that reason may be, but one possibility is that no priest was available, so a deacon baptized the adult.

In that rare case, after the adults have been baptized, the celebrant anoints them with chrism before clothing them in a white garment (OCIA 224; RCIA 228). The same may happen during the initiation of children of catechetical age (OCIA 358; RCIA 319) or in the exceptional circumstance

---

13. See *Liturgy and Life Study Bible* (Collegeville, MN: Liturgical Press, forthcoming [2022]).

when the celebrant administers the simpler order of adult initiation (OCIA 263), though this last option does not appear in the 1988 English translation.

This postbaptismal anointing of adults with chrism always indicates that something has gone wrong, and confirmation is not administered. However, it still confers the important commission to share the ministry of Christ.

The Minister of Anointing

The priest or deacon who celebrates the baptism of an infant is the usual minister of anointing with chrism.[14] In cases where the number of children is large and extra priests or deacons are present, these ministers may help anoint, even in the rare case of the postbaptismal anointing of adults.[15]

When a bishop presides at the baptism of an infant, the postbaptismal anointing is best conferred by a priest, preferably the pastor (CB 432, 444). As with the prebaptismal anointing, this highlights the baptism performed by the bishop and avoids any confusion between the postbaptismal anointing with chrism and the sacrament of confirmation.

In the absence of a priest, the bishop performs these rituals. They are not assigned to a deacon.

Whenever possible, then, the liturgy keeps the postbaptismal christological anointing associated with the ministry of priests. This agrees with some of the earliest testimony about baptismal practices in the Roman Rite.

The Formula of Anointing

The priest or deacon recites this formula when anointing with chrism after a baptism: "Almighty God, the Father of

---

14. OBC 62, for example.
15. OBC 62 and OCIA 224 (RCIA 228), for example.

our Lord Jesus Christ has freed you from sin, given you new birth by water and the Holy Spirit, and joined you to his people. He now anoints you with the Chrism of salvation, so that you may remain members of Christ, Priest, Prophet and King, unto eternal life."[16]

The formula slightly expands the one in force before the revisions stemming from Vatican II. That one used a different form of the verb: "May he anoint you," rather than "He anoints you." The word "now" is not explicit in the Latin, but it is implied because of the changed verb. The results of the anointing are immediate. Both versions of the formula use the Latin pronoun *ipse* to show that the subject of the sentence is doing the anointing: God the Father, not Jesus Christ. ICEL thought that inserting the word "now" also helped make that clear.

More significantly, the previous formula concluded more abruptly: "may he anoint you with the Chrism of salvation in the same Jesus Christ our Lord unto eternal life." The revised formula adds more purpose to the anointing. The oil aims to help the newly baptized "remain members of Christ" throughout their lives.

Furthermore, they will be members of Christ under his titles of priest, prophet, and king. This spells out the implication of the concise description in the previous line, that the newly baptized are joined to "his people." A fuller translation would express that they are joined to "the People of God." Thus the formula presumes the rich belief that God, who chose the children of Abraham for a covenant, has chosen a new people for a new covenant. The newly baptized enter this relationship as a royal priesthood, sharing through this anointing in the full ministry of Christ.

16. OBC 62, for example.

The revised formula calls to mind Vatican II's Dogmatic Constitution on the Church. The complete document explores the hierarchical levels of the church, but first it considers the church as a whole. The title of the second chapter is "The People of God." It builds on the popular verse from the First Letter of Peter (2:9) and explores how it is that all who follow Christ share in his priestly, prophetic, and royal office.[17] The postbaptismal anointing with chrism, which has its origins in a third-century practice, uses a formula enriched with twentieth-century insights.

ICEL could not unravel one potential difficulty. Both in Latin and in English, the formula opens with words that sound like the start of a prayer: "Almighty God." However, the minister does not say these words to God but to the person being anointed, declaring what God has done. With practice, though, the minister will know how to read it.

The declaration begins unusually with a double title: God is called both Almighty and Father. Then it specifies two great deeds of God: As Father, God has bestowed on the newly baptized a new birth; as Almighty, God has joined the newly baptized to the People of God. Both titles are part of the older formula and show the broad effects of this anointing.

Not Anointing Immediately before Confirmation

In some instances, the liturgy omits the postbaptismal anointing with chrism. Most notably, this happens when a priest baptizes an adult or a child of catechetical age. In that case, canon law gives him the faculty to confirm and obliges

17. Dogmatic Constitution on the Church, *Lumen Gentium*, Solemnly Proclaimed by His Holiness Paul VI on November 21, 1964, https://www.vatican.va/archive/hist_councils/ii_vatican_council/documents/vat-ii_const_19641121_lumen-gentium_en.html.

him to confirm for the benefit of the person he baptizes.[18] Some priests erroneously omit the confirmation of a newly baptized child of catechetical age, thinking the child must first attain the age for the confirmation of other children baptized as infants. However, the law obliges the priest to confirm a child he baptizes if that child has reached or surpassed approximately the age of First Communion.

The priest in this case omits the anointing with chrism that would have followed baptism. This avoids using the same oil on the same head within a matter of minutes, which could make it difficult for people to distinguish its purposes.

The anointings are different: The first, on the crown of the head, concerns Christ; confirmation on the forehead concerns the Holy Spirit. However, when baptism and confirmation take place in the same ceremony, the first anointing with chrism is omitted in favor of the second.[19] This is true of both adults and children of catechetical age.

The omission of the first oil may cause some disappointment. After all, everyone who is baptized shares in the priestly, prophetic, and royal ministry of Jesus Christ, so an anointing would underline that calling. The calling remains, even without its ritual expression.

Not Anointing in Danger of Death

If death seems imminent, baptism is the most important rite to offer. Especially when the patient is a newborn, the peril causes great distress for family, friends, medical professionals, and ministers. All wish to save the life of the child. At times, the best one can do is to confer the gift of spiritual life.

---

18. Canons 883 §2 and 885 §2.
19. OCIA 35, 223, 357; RCIA 216, 223, 318.

In a state of emergency, anyone may baptize. Even a non-believer may conduct the ceremony in accordance with the wishes of those responsible or of the person in danger. In the case of an unbaptized adult in danger of death, a layperson can find the proper ceremony in the same book that priests and deacons use for Christian initiation (OCIA 280; RCIA 372). When a layperson baptizes, no anointing with chrism may take place. However, a priest or deacon in this situation may anoint, otherwise following the same ceremony, a shorter order to be used in danger of death.

Usually, a priest who baptizes an adult in emergency also confirms if he has time and if he has chrism, omitting the postbaptismal anointing (OCIA 293; RCIA 388). Even in the case of an infant in danger of death, the priest omits the postbaptismal anointing and confirms (OBC 22).

If the minister of an emergency baptism is a deacon, if he has time, and if he has chrism, he gives the postbaptismal anointing.[20] A priest or deacon may omit chrism altogether in favor of using the small amount of time available to ensure baptism (OCIA 281; RCIA 373).

In the case of an infant who received an emergency baptism, if the child recovers, all will praise God. The ceremonies that had been omitted may be conducted in accordance with the Order of Bringing a Baptized Child to the Church (OBC 165). These include the postbaptismal anointing with chrism (OBC 178). As beautiful as the anointing is, if time is of the essence, baptism alone suffices.

---

20. OCIA 291; RCIA 385, where the rubric appears one paragraph later than in the typical edition.

Not Anointing When a Catechist Baptizes

In some parts of the world, priests and deacons are so scarce that bishops may depute certain catechists to baptize. Vatican II made provision for this especially in mission lands.[21] The Order of Baptism of Children includes the ceremony for them to follow.

Because they are laypersons, catechists omit certain parts of the ceremony, including the anointing with chrism (OBC 20). However, the catechist or other layperson who presides recites a version of the postbaptismal prayer, without mentioning the oil: "May almighty God, the Father of our Lord Jesus Christ, who has freed you from sin, given you new birth by water and the Holy Spirit, and joined you to his people, grant that as you have now been made Christians, you may remain members of Christ, Priest, Prophet and King, unto eternal life" (OBC 151).

Thus, even without receiving a physical anointing with chrism, the newly baptized person still participates in the ministry of Christ.

The council authorized this ceremony for situations where the absence of priests and deacons is so chronic that the local church has no immediate hope for remedy. Awful to consider among nations richer in clergy, the ceremony could become necessary if some tragedy caused the incapacity or death of many priests. If such an unthinkable situation ever befell a community, the laity accepting the responsibility to baptize would already have access to the necessary ceremony, found in chapter IV of the Order of Baptism of Children: "Order of Baptism of Children to be Used by Catechists in the Absence of a Priest or Deacon" (OBC 132). Although laity

---

21. Constitution on the Sacred Liturgy, *Sacrosanctum Concilium*, Solemnly Promulgated by His Holiness Paul VI on December 4, 1963, 68.

may not anoint with chrism, they may confer what is essential: baptism.

Not Anointing a Large Group

The church envisions one more scenario in which priests and deacons authorized to anoint with chrism may omit it. In this case, the reason is a happy problem: The number of those to be baptized is simply huge. One hears stories of missionary saints who baptized hundreds of thousands of people in their career. The Order of Baptism of Children actually includes a ceremony in which the number of infants is so great that the ministers somehow have to reduce the ritual elements (OBC 107).

In the typical edition of the Order of Baptism of Children, the Vatican permits the omission of anointing with chrism in this circumstance (OBC 24 §4). This keeps the minister from having to approach each baptized child a second time. Families may provide the white garment and assist with the lighted candle without the minister's direct involvement for each child (OBC 126, 127).

However, in the United States, the bishops have judged that this circumstance does not exist. The number of children to be baptized is never so large that the priest or deacon is physically unable to anoint each child. Therefore, outside the danger of death, the postbaptismal anointing is not to be omitted in the United States, no matter the number of children (OBC 24 §4, 125). The celebrant may, however, say the formula only once while anointing many.

The postbaptismal anointing with chrism beautifully expresses one meaning of baptism, a sharing in the mission of Christ who is priest, prophet, and king. At times the minister omits this meaningful ceremony in favor of two others that rank ahead of it: baptism and confirmation. Nonetheless, the effects of baptism always include what this anointing proclaims.

Confirmation

Confirmation as Conformation

When those who have been baptized are anointed with chrism in the sacrament of confirmation, they "receive the indelible character, the seal of the Lord, together with the gift of the Spirit that conforms them more fully to Christ and gives them the grace of spreading among men and women 'the pleasing fragrance of Christ.' "[22] This explanation comes from the introduction to the Order of Confirmation.

At the initiation of adults, confirmation forms a unit with baptism. Together they connect the mission of the Son with the outpouring of the Holy Spirit. In the unity of these two sacraments the entire Trinity comes to the newly baptized (OCIA 34; RCIA 215).

Although chrism is the oil for the postbaptismal anointing of infants, its administration in confirmation enjoys the higher rank of accomplishing a new sacrament. One result is conformation to Christ.

In the bishop's sample homily at a confirmation ceremony, he explains that this conformation is to Christ as he was anointed by the Holy Spirit at his baptism. From that anointing, Christ "was sent forth for the work of his ministry, to pour out on the earth the fire of the same Spirit" (OConf 22). The candidates are conformed to Christ not just in identity but also in mission. The newly confirmed are sent forth to share the Spirit they have received.

In the moments before laying hands on the candidates, usually by extending his hands over the entire group, the bishop begs all the faithful to join him in prayer. He asks that the Holy

---

22. *The Order of Confirmation* [OConf] (Washington DC: United States Conference of Catholic Bishops, 2016), 9.

Spirit will "through his holy anointing conform [the candidates] more fully to Christ, the Son of God" (OConf 24).

In adult initiation, the priest catechizes the ones he just baptized concerning confirmation: "you also are to receive the promised power of the Holy Spirit, so that, being more perfectly conformed to Christ, you may bear witness to the Lord's Passion and Resurrection."[23] The priest then addresses the entire assembly, inviting them to pray, just as a bishop does when he celebrates confirmation apart from baptism. Here, too, the priest asks for prayers that this anointing may conform the newly baptized more fully to Christ.

During a confirmation Mass, both options for the prayer over the offerings mention this conformation. In the first, the bishop prays that those who are "conformed more perfectly" to the Son of God "may grow steadily in bearing witness to him" (OConf 58). In the second, he prays that those signed "with a spiritual anointing. . . may constantly offer themselves" in union with Christ (59). As Christ offered himself to the Father from the cross, so those conformed to Christ by this anointing offer themselves to the Father by sharing the mission of evangelization.

People rightly associate the meaning of confirmation with the outpouring of the Holy Spirit. However, the liturgy also associates the anointing with a participation in the anointing of Christ. He was anointed with the Spirit at his baptism to begin his mission in the world. The candidates are anointed with the Spirit at their confirmation for the same missionary purpose. The anointing conforms them to Christ.

---

23. OCIA 229; see RCIA 233, but this translation comes from the OConf.

Occasion for Confirmation

Confirmation may be administered on a variety of occasions. At the initiation of adults and of children of catechetical age, the priest who baptizes is obliged to confirm.[24] Catholics baptized as infants usually receive confirmation at a later date when they have the use of reason and are suitably instructed, properly disposed, and able to renew their baptismal promises.[25] A priest who receives into the full communion of the Catholic Church a validly baptized Christian confers confirmation in the same ceremony.[26] A priest may confirm any baptized Catholic in danger of death, including an infant he has just baptized.[27]

Although the sacrament may be conferred in all these instances, the meaning of the anointing remains constant. It conforms the confirmed to Christ, empowering them to bear witness in the world.

The Minister of Confirmation

The ordinary minister of confirmation is the bishop. On some occasions a priest may confirm.[28]

The association of the bishop with this sacrament pertains to a long tradition stemming from his role in initiation. Bishops are the spiritual fathers of their dioceses, a role they perform eloquently when they baptize, confirm, and offer communion to new adult Christians. When priests and

24. Canons 883 §2 and 885 §2.

25. Canon 889 §2.

26. Rite of Reception of Baptized Christians into the Full Communion of the Catholic Church 17; RCIA 493. This does not apply to the rare instances with the priest receives someone with a valid confirmation, such as chrismation in an Eastern Orthodox Church.

27. Canons 883 §3, 889 §2, and 891.

28. Canon 882.

deacons began to share the ministry of baptism in the West, bishops reserved confirmation to themselves, retaining some expression of their spiritual fatherhood. The beginnings of this shift can be traced to the third century, but settled more decisively in the fifth.[29]

About the same time the church searched the New Testament for biblical roots to the practice that had developed: confirmation separate from baptism, celebrated by a bishop. The Bible offers no evidence that the apostles anointed the newly baptized. Nonetheless, it does bear witness to the practice of laying hands on candidates for the gift of the Holy Spirit.

Traditionally, the church has seen confirmation as an extension of the ministry of the apostles Peter and John in Samaria (Acts 8:14-17) and of the apostle Paul in Ephesus (Acts 19:1-7). Both these exceptional instances concern small groups of Christians who had experienced baptism but not the gift of the Holy Spirit. The apostles remedied the situation through imposing hands and conferring the Holy Spirit upon them. Because the church sees bishops as successors of the apostles, this biblical testimony is sometimes used to explain the association of confirmation with the ministry of bishops in the Catholic Church.

Even so, priests are expected to confirm adults and children of catechetical age whom they baptize or those validly baptized in another denomination whom they receive into the full communion of the Catholic Church.[30] Priests may also confirm when the candidate is in danger of death.[31]

---

29. Paul Turner, *Ages of Initiation: The First Two Christian Millennia* (Collegeville, MN: Liturgical Press, 2000), 51.

30. Canons 883 §2 and 885 §2.

31. Canon 883 §3.

Usually a priest does not confirm those who were baptized Catholics as infants. However, a bishop may delegate a priest to do so either in his stead or together with him in case of necessity,[32] such as occasions when a bishop is unable to be present or when the group of candidates is large.

If priests assist the bishop in administering confirmation, they join him in the prayer for the gift of the Holy Spirit by raising their hands over the group while the bishop alone recites the words (OConf 25). When the moment to anoint arrives, the bishop hands each priest a vessel of chrism. Concelebrants who do not administer confirmation with the bishop do not raise their hands while he prays.

One would expect priests who anoint to concelebrate the confirmation Mass with the bishop. However, if they do not, or if confirmation is administered outside of Mass, then the priests who confirm wear a stole over a surplice and cassock, or over an alb, and they may also wear a cope (CB 458).

Even in these exceptional circumstances when a priest confirms, chrism always comes from the bishop.[33] Only a bishop may consecrate it. A priest confirms as an ambassador by means of his ordination, his actions, and the chrism that he uses.

Anointing and Handlaying

To anoint, "The bishop dips the tip of the thumb of his right hand in the Chrism and, with the thumb, makes the Sign of the Cross on the forehead of the one to be confirmed" as he recites the formula (OConf 27). A priest confirms in the same way.

---

32. Canon 884 §1 and 2.
33. Canon 880 §2.

The action calls to mind various passages from the New Testament. Paul reminds the Ephesians that they have been "marked with the seal of the promised Holy Spirit" (1:13). The First Letter of John affirms that Christians "have been anointed by the Holy One" and that the anointing that they received "abides" in them and "teaches" them (2:20, 27). If these passages apply the concepts of seal and anointing figuratively, they still explain how within a short while Christians began incorporating a physical anointing into their initiation rites.

Many people witnessing a confirmation ceremony conclude that the laying on of hands happens when the bishop extends his hands over the group to be confirmed and recites the prayer for the sevenfold gift of the Holy Spirit. Even the ritual book carries the subheading "The Laying on of Hands" for this part of the ceremony (OConf 24).

However, Pope Saint Paul VI declared that "the anointing with chrism on the forehead. . . is done by the laying on of the hand."[34] This is restated in the Code of Canon Law.[35] As the bishop or priest applies the chrism to the forehead, the action constitutes the sacramental handlaying. As they anoint with their thumb, some bishops place the rest of their hand on the top of the candidate's head to exemplify the handlaying on each person. Others simply apply the chrism with the thumb without involving the rest of their hand. It does not matter; in either way, the anointing itself constitutes the handlaying.

During 2020 amidst the pandemic, some bishops wondered if they could confirm without touching the candidate

---

34. Pope Paul VI, Apostolic Constitution on the Sacrament of Confirmation, August 15, 1971.
35. Canon 880 §1.

at all, taking a step to stem the possible spread of the contagion. Canon law permits the use of an instrument in the case of anointing the sick,[36] but it is silent about administering the other oils in this way. The Vatican's Congregation for Divine Worship and the Discipline of the Sacraments received a formal question, a *dubium*, from the USCCB. The bishops asked if the use of the thumb was essential to administering the sacrament. They received this response: "The use by the minister of an instrument (gloves, cotton swab. . .), does not affect the validity of the Sacrament."[37] Although this seems to remove even further the symbolism of the imposition of hands, the action of anointing still implies it. An instrument may save lives as it confers grace.

Formula

While administering the anointing, the bishop or priest calls the candidate by name and recites the formula, "be sealed with the Gift of the Holy Spirit" (OConf 27). Because the handlaying is enclosed within the anointing, and because the bishop prayed at the chrism Mass that the Spirit come especially upon this oil, the formula directly proclaims that the Holy Spirit seals the candidate. This is not the first time that the candidate has received the Holy Spirit. That happened at baptism. But this sacrament seals the candidate with the gift of the Spirit.

As baptism does, so confirmation imparts an indelible character, indicating that the sacrament can never be repeated. Its effects are everlasting. One is therefore sealed with it. The Code of Canon law expresses the meaning of the sacrament in similar terms: It impresses a character by

---

36. Canon 1000 §2.
37. Leonard P. Blair, "Memorandum," June 8, 2020.

which the gift of the Holy Spirit enriches the baptized, obliging them to be stronger witnesses of Christ.[38] Although some popular piety wrongly associates confirmation with a candidate's personal appropriation of the faith, the sacrament is a gift of the Spirit to assist making a candidate a stronger witness to Christ.

Prior to the revisions of Vatican II, the formula pertained more directly to the oil and to the bishop. He said always in Latin, "I sign you with the sign of the cross, and I confirm you with the chrism of salvation. In the name of the Father, and of the Son, and of the Holy Spirit." The revised formula expresses instead the effects of confirmation.

Confirmation in Danger of Death

Any priest may administer confirmation to a candidate in danger of death. Permission for this is even recorded in the ritual book for the pastoral care of the sick (AS 31; PCS 31). In an emergency, he may be thinking more about the oil of the sick than the oil of chrism, so the rubrics reminds him of other potential pastoral concerns.

If the candidate has never been baptized, a priest administers both baptism and confirmation. The order of initiation of adults contains a short ritual to help him (OCIA 278; RCIA 370). He introduces the sacrament of confirmation with only some of the words from its normal administration in adult initiation (OCIA 229; RCIA 233). In this case, he does not declare that the sacrament will enable the candidate to bear witness to the Lord's passion and resurrection, nor to become an active member of the church to build up the body of Christ in faith and charity (OCIA 293; RCIA 389). Sadly, the priest is aware that death is likely imminent, and the opportunities

38. Canon 879.

for bearing witness and building up the church are few. Of course, any dying Christian bears witness to the Lord's passion and resurrection, and any dying Christian can build up the church through accepting the grace of the moment. The words of the priest at this time are circumspect.

If the dying person has already been baptized but has never been confirmed, any priest may confirm. This applies also to a child who has not yet reached the use of reason (OConf 52).

If time permits, the priest celebrates the entire confirmation ceremony; otherwise, he makes it extremely brief: He lays hands over the sick person and recites the prayer for the sevenfold gift of the Holy Spirit (OConf 54). Then he anoints the forehead with chrism while reciting the formula (55). In cases of extreme necessity, when he does not even have time for all those components, he limits the ceremony to the anointing with chrism while speaking the formula (56).

These permissions show the care that the church offers to those experiencing crisis, the desire to share the fruits of the sacraments with those who cannot otherwise prepare themselves more properly. Confirmation is a sealing with the gift of the Holy Spirit. The church desires every Catholic to receive its benefits.

Reception into the Full Communion of the Catholic Church

The Candidate

A person who has been validly baptized in another ecclesial community and wishes to become a Catholic is prepared and received appropriately. Confirmation is usually part of the celebration. Only those with a valid confirmation, such as members of Eastern Orthodox Churches, are not to be confirmed. Those who have experienced a confirmation within other Western Christian denominations are confirmed in this ceremony. The Catholic Church regards confirmation as a sacrament; other denominations do not. The church requires that confirmation be administered by an ordained Catholic bishop or priest.

The ceremony is called a reception into the full communion of the Catholic Church. It is technically not a "communion with the Catholic Church," as though the person remains somehow outside the church but experiences communion with it. It is a reception into the fullness "of" communion that the Catholic Church represents.

The reception happens after the candidate professes the Nicene Creed and declares acceptance of what the Catholic Church teaches. The priest declares that the Lord receives the candidate into the Catholic Church, giving full communion.[39]

Confirmation follows.[40] Sometimes people who experienced this ceremony say, "I was confirmed a Catholic," as if confirmation made them Catholic. However, the rite of reception made them Catholic. Then, as Catholics, they were confirmed.

Meaning

The fundamental meaning of confirmation does not change. The candidate is sealed with the gift of the Holy Spirit for the purpose of bearing witness. The formula is the same, as is the process of anointing.

Nonetheless, the candidate undergoes this ceremony before receiving First Communion in the same Mass. Confirmation effectively consecrates the candidate with gifts of the Holy Spirit to foster a worthy reception of Holy Com-

---

39. OCIA Rite of Reception 16; RCIA 492.
40. OCIA Rite of Reception 17; RCIA 493–94.

munion. Because of the validity of the person's baptism in another denomination, the candidate began the process of Christian initiation much earlier than this ceremony. Nonetheless, the church still regards confirmation in this instance as a sacrament of initiation, conferred through anointing with chrism.

Ordination

The Ordination of a Priest

An anointing of the Holy Spirit sets certain men apart as ordained priests in the Catholic Church. The introduction to the ritual uses this expression in a quote from Vatican II: "by the anointing of the Holy Spirit, they are signed with a special character and are so configured to Christ the Priest that they have the power to act in the person of Christ the Head."[41]

A physical anointing with chrism forms only one part of the ordination ceremony, but the overall effect of the entire rite is an anointing with the Holy Spirit. The Bible's only explicit references to anointing with the Holy Spirit are in the community's prayer after Peter and John were released from prison, and Peter's description of the baptism of Jesus in the Jordan (Acts 4:27; 10:38). As Jesus was anointed in the Spirit, so is a priest as he shares in the ministry of Christ, the Anointed One.

41. Rites of Ordination of a Bishop, of Priests, and of Deacons [OBP], *The Roman Pontifical* (Vatican City: Vox Clara Committee, 2012), 101, citing Second Vatican Council, Decree on the Ministry and Life of Priests, *Presbyterorum Ordinis* 2.

Ordination imparts a character and therefore cannot be repeated.[42] The same is true of baptism and confirmation.

Every baptized Christian shares in the priestly, prophetic, and royal ministry of Jesus Christ, but the ordination ceremony underscores the particularly priestly role of the man receiving this sacrament. He will offer the sacrifice, performing a priestly function, every time he presides at Mass. As he celebrates the Mass and other sacraments, he will praise God and pray for others—both priestly functions. Other Christian denominations have services that resemble the Mass in offering eucharistic praise or sharing communion from the Lord's Supper, but Catholics uniquely call the eucharistic celebration a sacrifice, for which the presider is called a priest. Because priesthood is one way to describe the ministry of Christ, it becomes the way the church describes the one who acts in the place of Christ the Priest and Head of the assembly gathered at prayer.

The preface for the ordination Mass of any bishop, priest, or deacon, is the one for the chrism Mass as well (OBP 343). It notes two uses of chrism: one in the rites of initiation, and the other in the rites of ordination. The foundation for both of these is the spiritual anointing of Jesus at his baptism in the waters of the Jordan. Christ adorns all the baptized with a share in his royal priesthood, but he also "chooses men to become sharers in his sacred ministry through the laying on of hands." The preface continues to proclaim that these ordained ministers preside at the Eucharist, lead God's people in charity, nourish them with the Word, and strengthen them with sacraments.

The Latin word for "men" in this preface is *homines*, which is gender-inclusive, but the English translation renders it

42. Canon 845 §1.

gender-specific in conformity with the law that only males may be ordained.[43]

The preface concludes by proclaiming the spirit with which ordained ministers carry out these responsibilities: "As they give up their lives for you and for the salvation of their brothers and sisters, they strive to be conformed to the image of Christ himself and offer you a constant witness of faith and love." The preface borrows imagery from the order of confirmation as if the grace of that sacrament continues to operate in their ordained ministry. At confirmation, the anointing with chrism conformed them to Christ and commissioned them to bear witness to the Spirit. They channel the fruits of confirmation into a new ministry.

Although anointing is the symbol of priesthood, the sacrament is conferred when the bishop lays hands on the candidates and offers the prayer of ordination.

Biblical References

The ordination ceremony draws inspiration from many passages in the Bible. The prayer of ordination builds its case from the old covenant to the new. It praises God for establishing offices through mystical rites; the book of Exodus in particular describes the elaborate ceremony that consecrated Aaron and his sons as priests, in which God asked Moses to pour oil on the head of Aaron (29:7). The letter to the Hebrews calls Jesus both apostle and high priest (3:1), bringing to fulfillment this priesthood of Aaron. As high priest, Christ entered the holy place not annually, but only once; and he offered not the blood of goats and calves, but his own blood (Heb 9:11-12). At the Last Supper, Jesus had consecrated his apostles in the truth (John 17:17), making them sharers

43. Canon 1024.

in his mission. The prayer of ordination therefore affirms that Jesus Christ brought the priesthood of the Old Testament to its fulfillment and shares that priesthood with those followers whom he appoints as leaders. That priesthood will be symbolized with an anointing.

The preface similarly explores the imagery of anointing through biblical testimony. It opens by calling the baptism of Jesus his anointing of the Holy Spirit (Acts 10:38). Drawing on the prophetic testimony in the book of Psalms concerning Melchizedek (Ps 110:4), the letter to the Hebrews calls Jesus the one who holds his priesthood permanently (Heb 5:5-6; 6:20; 7:17-24). The preface calls Jesus the "High Priest of the new and eternal covenant," whose "one Priesthood should continue in the Church."

The entrance antiphon of the ordination Mass makes a different allusion to anointing. It refers to the account of Jesus entering the synagogue in Nazareth at the beginning of his public ministry and reading from the book of the prophet Isaiah: "The Spirit of the Lord is upon me, for he has anointed me and sent me to preach the good news to the poor, to heal the broken-hearted" (OBP 342). The anointing shows that the priest not only shares a title with Christ, but also the responsibility to act on behalf of the poor and brokenhearted. As the anointed one, the priest is to share good news and to heal.

Anointing the Hands

When the bishop anoints the hands of the new priest, he imports all this imagery to the action. The sacristan prepares for this moment by making chrism ready before the ceremony begins (OBP 115d).

After the bishop lays hands on the candidate and recites the prayer of ordination, the new priest puts on his proper vestments for the first time. Then come additional symbols of his office. According to the introduction to the ceremony, the anointing of the hands signifies the man's participation in the priesthood of Christ (OBP 113).

The anointing immediately follows the vesting of the new priest, showing that not only the clothes on his body, but also the oil on his skin, identify him with Christ the priest. In the ritual book, the subhead for this part of the ceremony conjoins two actions: the anointing of hands and the handing on of bread and wine (OBP 132).

The new priest kneels before the bishop (CB 535). This has a practical value, making the anointing easier to administer. It also places the priest in a position associated with humility and prayer.

Using chrism, the bishop anoints the priest's palms. He will imitate Christ in many ways; his entire ministry is an anointing in the Holy Spirit. However, his priestly actions pertain to offering sacrifice with his hands. In praying over this anointing, the bishop recalls that the Father anointed Jesus with the Holy Spirit and power at his baptism, as Peter explained to the household of Cornelius (Acts 10:38). He prays that through this anointing God will "guard and preserve" the new priest. The Latin original uses only one verb, *custodiat*, but ICEL felt that two words better expressed the richness of its meaning. The bishop prays that God will "guard" the new priest from harm and "preserve" him in his ministry.

The bishop prays that with this divine protection, the new priest "may sanctify the Christian people and offer sacrifice to God" (OBP 133). At the Last Supper, Jesus prayed that the Father would sanctify his followers (John 17:17), and at the anointing of hands, when the new priest is himself being sanctified, he is instructed to sanctify the people as well. He will also offer sacrifice to God, the duty of any priest.

The first items these newly anointed hands touch are the vessels holding the bread and wine for the offering of the ordination Mass. Some of the faithful present these to a deacon, who gives them to the bishop, who entrusts them into the hands of the new priest. The bishop instructs him to imitate these elements, making his own life a sacrifice (OBP 135).

This action is unusual. Usually upon receiving the gifts, the presider sets them on the altar. But on this occasion the bishop sets them first into the hands of the new priest, showing with clarity what happens at every Mass: the priest aligns himself with the bread and wine as a sacrifice to God. Before the washing of the hands, he prays, "With humble spirit and contrite heart / may we be accepted by you, O Lord."[44] Then he incenses the gifts, and a minister incenses the priest. The newly ordained will serve at every Mass both as priest and as sacrifice.

The antiphon that the community may sing at this time draws these themes together. Inspired by the letter to the Hebrews (Heb 7:17), it applies the appearance of Melchizedek in the book of Psalms to Jesus (Ps 110:4). It also remembers Melchizedek's dual role in the book of Genesis: a king who blessed Abraham and a priest who brought out bread and wine (Gen 14:18). At the ordination Mass, as the new priest is vested, anointed, and presented with bread and wine, the community chants this biblical testimony showing how this priest participates in the high priesthood of Jesus Christ, the priest forever.

Some ordination greeting cards mistakenly assume that the candidate is becoming a priest forever in the line of Melchizedek. But that is who Christ is. The ordained man

---

44. Roman Missal, Order of Mass 26.

will remain a priest because of the everlasting character of this sacrament, but the eternal priesthood belongs to Jesus, the Messiah, the Anointed One, the High Priest of the new covenant.

The Ordination of a Bishop

After the Vatican chooses a particular priest to become a bishop, he participates in an elaborate ordination ceremony, usually at his new cathedral. One element is the anointing of his head with chrism. This symbolizes his distinctive share in the priesthood of Jesus Christ (OBP 26).

Before this Mass begins, various elements need to be prepared. These include sacred chrism (OBP 28d, 65d). The vessel of oil may be set on the credence table or some auxiliary table, accessible for the moment when it is needed.

As the ordination ceremony begins, all may sing a hymn such as *Veni, Creator Spiritus* (OBP 35, 71). This includes a lyric that calls the Holy Spirit "the soul's anointing from above" (OBP Appendix I). It prepares the community in advance to witness a new outpouring of the Holy Spirit upon one who has already been anointed in confirmation.

The anointing of the new bishop takes place just after the prayer of ordination. The principal ordaining bishop puts on a linen gremial, his ceremonial apron. The newly ordained bishop kneels before him. The ordaining bishop anoints the new bishop's head with chrism. He usually pours out the oil from a vessel over the new bishop's head. It can get messy.

As he performs this action, the ordaining bishop prays that God will pour upon the new bishop "the oil of mystical anointing," so that an abundance of God's blessings will make him fruitful (OBP 49, 85; CB 586). Even if only a small amount of oil touches the new bishop's head, he receives a "mystical" anointing—one that touches every aspect of his ministry. The letter to the Hebrews calls Jesus Christ the high priest (4:14-16), a position historically inaugurated through the pouring of oil. Here the bishop receives a physical anointing to participate in this mystical anointing of Christ as priest.

Ordination imparts a character and cannot be repeated.[45] However, some men participate in more than one of the different grades of orders: deacon, priest, and bishop. These are conferred by the imposition of hands and the prayer of consecration.[46]

Chrism therefore is an auxiliary sign of this indelible character. The anointing of a bishop does not constitute the administration of the sacrament, as anointing does in the case of confirmation and of the sacrament of the sick. Rather, it illustrates his new ministry.

The Dedication of a Church and an Altar

New Church, New Altar

Chrism will anoint the walls of a new church and the top of any new altar, even one placed in a previously dedicated church. The bishop still comes to dedicate each new church and each new altar.

As the sacristans arrange items for the dedication of an altar, they prepare a special place in the sacristy, the sanctuary, or the nave for the vessels containing chrism.[47]

The Order of the Dedication recommends this antiphon for the entrance: "Turn your eyes, O God, our shield, and

---

45. Canon 1008.
46. Canon 1009 §1 and 2.
47. *The Order of the Dedication of a Church and an Altar* [ODC] (Washington, DC: United States Conference of Catholic Bishops, 2018), chap. II, "The Order of the Dedication of a Church," 21b.

look on the face of your Anointed One; one day within your courts is better than a thousand elsewhere." That antiphon comes from Psalm 84 (vv. 10-11), but it pairs with Psalm 43, which speaks of coming to the altar of God, who is joy and gladness.[48]

A Christian interpretation of that psalm on this occasion imagines the community asking the Father to see the face of the Son in the new altar of a church dedicated eternally for worship.

Some symbols in the dedication of a new church resemble ones for Christian initiation. The people may gather outside the door of the church (ODC chap. II, 29), as they do for the rite of acceptance into the order of catechumens (OCIA 73; RCIA 48). The bishop blesses water and sprinkles it on the people, the walls and the altar (ODC chap. II, 48–49), recalling the mystery of baptism. The community prays a Litany of Supplication, invoking the aid of the saints (chap. II, 57–60). The altar and walls are anointed with chrism (chap. II, 63–65). The altar is covered in a white cloth (chap. II, 69). The candles of the church are set ablaze (chap II, 70–71). At the climax of the celebration, the Eucharist is shared (chap. II, 72–78). All these symbols overlap with those in the rites of initiation.

The new church and altar are celebrating their own initiation. They are set apart as something sacred in the eyes of God. They are places where the Holy Spirit will dwell and where the gospel will be proclaimed.

Prayer of Dedication of the Church

Before anointing the altar and walls of a new church, the bishop offers a solemn prayer for its dedication (ODC chap

---

48. ODC chap. IV, "The Order of the Dedication of an Altar," 33.

II, 62). He sets the purpose of this church against the image of the heavenly Jerusalem that the book of Revelation calls the bride of Christ (21:2). Recalling Jesus' image of the vine and the branches (John 15:5), he calls the church the Lord's chosen vine with branches that fill the world and reach toward heaven. Alluding to more biblical passages, the bishop calls the new church God's dwelling place among the human race (Rev 21:3), a temple built of living stones (1 Pet 2:5), and a structure standing upon the apostles with Christ Jesus as its cornerstone (Eph 2:20). It is the city set on a hill (Matt 5:14) that shines with the light of the Lamb (Rev 21:23-24).

The bishop then makes his principal petition, that God will pour forth his sanctifying power "upon this church and upon this altar, to make this for ever a holy place with a table always prepared for the Sacrifice of Christ." He continues praying that the new church may be a holy place where the divine grace of baptism overwhelms sin, the faithful celebrate the Eucharist, the praise of humans and angels resounds, "the poor find mercy, the oppressed attain true freedom, and all people [are] clothed with the dignity" of the children of God (ODC chap. II, 62).

That is the sacred purpose of the building that the bishop then anoints with sacred chrism.

Prayer of Dedication of the Altar

If an older church is receiving a new altar, the bishop offers a solemn prayer for its dedication (ODC chap. IV, 48). He recalls the archetypes of altars: Noah set one up to offer sacrifice after the flood (Gen 8:20-21). Abraham constructed an altar where he witnessed the sparing of his son Isaac (Gen 22:9-10). Moses built an altar and sprinkled upon it the blood of a sacrificial lamb (Exod 24:4, 6), prefiguring the cross, where Christ ruled as priest and victim.

The bishop then makes the main petition, asking God to pour forth "sanctifying power upon this altar, built in the house of the church, that it may be an altar dedicated for all time by the sacrifice of Christ, and stand as the Lord's table" where the people of God are refreshed at the divine banquet (ODC chap. IV, 48). He prays that it may be a sign of Christ, a festive table, the place of intimate communion with God, a place of peace, a source of unity, and the center of praise and thanksgiving.

He will anoint the altar for all these sacred purposes.

Anointing the Altar and the Walls

The bishop anoints the altar and walls of a new church with sacred chrism, linking the dedication to this action. In the sacraments of baptism, confirmation, and ordination, the church uses chrism partly to show that the anointed individual can never receive the same anointing again. In the dedication of a church and altar, this building and this object are sealed permanently for sacred use.

Just before anointing the altar, the bishop says, "May the Lord by his power sanctify this altar and this house, which by our ministry we anoint, so that as visible signs they may express the mystery of Christ and the Church."[49] The altar and the building express the mystery of Christ and the church, the bride and bridegroom who witness the increase and celebration of new divine life within the walls and upon the altar.

The bishop anoints the altar with chrism. He pours the sacred oil on the middle and on each of the four corners. He may stop there, but "it is praiseworthy for him to anoint the entire table with it" (ODC chap. II, 64; CB 946).

---

49. ODC chap. II, 64. If he anoints only the new altar in an older building, his introduction omits the reference to anointing the walls (chap. IV, 49).

If the bishop is anointing only a new altar in a previously dedicated church, the community may sing the prophetic verse from Psalm 45, "God, your God, has anointed you, above your companions with the oil of gladness" (v. 8; ODC chap. IV, 50). Originally composed for a royal wedding, the Christian community sings the same verse to Christ, whose presence this altar symbolizes.

In a new church, usually the wall locations have been predetermined and marked with crosses made of some suitable material or carved into the walls (ODC chap. II, 22). According to tradition, this building is an image of the holy city of Jerusalem from the book of Revelation, which has twelve gates, three on each of its four walls (21:12-14). For the anointing of a church, twelve places are prepared; however, if circumstances suggest, four places suffice (ODC chap. II, 16).

The bishop may share the task of anointing the walls with two or four of the concelebrating priests (ODC chap. II, 63, 64; CB 902, 903). If so, he presents the vessels of chrism to them. The ritual does not explain why a bishop may choose to involve others. It could pertain to the difficulty of reaching some locations without ladders, a desire to expedite the length of the ceremony, or symbolically to share ministry with the priests, especially if they have the pastoral care of those who will worship in the new building. For any reason, the bishop may even entrust the anointing of the walls completely to concelebrating priests (CB 902).

During the anointing, the people may sing a psalm of the loveliness of God's dwelling place (Ps 84), together with a New Testament refrain about God dwelling with the human race (Rev 21:3), or the holiness of God's own building (1 Cor 3:9), an image that Saint Paul uses to describe the people, not the structure (ODC chap. II, 64).

After the walls have been anointed, the new church's candles are lighted for the first time, including those set at the places on the walls that received an anointing (ODC chap. II, 71). The community may relight these candles on subsequent festive occasions, when they will help people recall the anointing of these sacred walls.

The Code of Canon Law clearly describes the results of anointing an altar. It is reserved exclusively for divine worship and entirely exempt from profane use.[50]

The Altar as Symbol of Christ

Many people witnessing such a dedication retain one especially vivid memory: the bishop anointing the altar with chrism. The unusual image of him slathering oil on top of the bare altar convinces participants that this furniture is now holy and explains why it is to be located "where it is truly the center toward which the attention of the whole congregation of the faithful naturally turns" (GIRM 299).

The Order of the Dedication of a Church and an Altar expresses the significance of this anointing: "By the anointing with Chrism the altar is made a symbol of Christ who, before all others, is and is called, 'The Anointed One'; for the Father anointed him with the Holy Spirit and constituted him High Priest, who on the altar of his Body would offer the sacrifice of his life for the salvation of all" (ODC chap. II, 16a).

This anointing explains why ministers show great respect to the altar in the ordinary celebration of Mass. The priest and deacon make a profound bow to the altar and kiss it at the beginning and end of the celebration (GIRM 49, 90d). The book of the Gospels is placed upon it (117, 122). Apart from this book, the cross, candles, and the missal, no other objects may rest there as Mass begins (117, 306). Ministers passing from one side of the sanctuary to the other or who enter and

---

50. Canon 1239 §1.

leave the sanctuary during the course of the Mass make their reverence to the altar (CB 72). The priest may incense the altar during the entrance chant and again during the preparation of the gifts, incensing the crucifix together with the altar both times (GIRM 276). The altar symbolizes Christ.

Some Catholics are surprised to learn that during the course of the Mass no genuflections are made to the tabernacle (GIRM 274). Even if the tabernacle is located in the sanctuary, once the Mass is underway, the altar becomes the center of attention. The altar is the locus of the eucharistic prayer and the source for communion.

The Mensa

The top of the altar is called the mensa. The entire altar is sacred, but the action of the Eucharist transpires on its top, which has a special name and purpose.

The GIRM uses the Latin word *mensa* several times, and the English translation usually calls it a "table," but in Latin it specifically means the tabletop. Traditionally, the mensa is stone (GIRM 301). Some churches with wooden altars have placed a stone in the top center to honor this tradition. However, a bishops' conference may permit other materials that are dignified and solid.

The altar of sacrifice is also the table of the Lord, the *mensa*, where the people participate at Mass and give thanks for the Eucharist (GIRM 296). The people present for the Mass form one body partly "by participating together at the Lord's table," a poetic expression for the sharing of communion (96).

Therefore the GIRM limits items that may be placed upon the mensa for the Liturgy of the Eucharist: the chalice and paten, ciboria, corporal, purificator, pall, and missal (73, 306). Flowers may be placed *around* the altar, but not *on* the mensa (305). The collection is to be put "in a suitable place away from the Eucharistic table" (73), which means off the mensa, not at a distance from the entire altar.

All these explanations underscore the sacred purpose of the mensa, which the bishop has anointed. He seals the mensa with sacred chrism.

By analogy, the GIRM refers to the ambo as the mensa of the Word (GIRM 28, 57, 355). The English translation each time calls it "the table of the Word." The bishop does not anoint an ambo, but that mensa serves people the feast of Sacred Scripture as the mensa of the altar serves the feast of the Eucharist.

When the GIRM instructs how to celebrate the Eucharist outside a sacred place, it declares that a suitable table may be used (297). Although it uses the word mensa, here it means any table, such as one temporarily set up in the common room of a nursing home, one that has never been consecrated.

Otherwise, a mensa is a consecrated tabletop that deserves respect at all times. Even when Mass is not being celebrated, people should take care that the mensa does not become a resting place for photography equipment or a staging area for flower arrangements, for example. It has been anointed for a more honorable purpose.

The Permanence of the Dedication

The dedication of a church and altar is permanent. However, at times of tragedy, either may be damaged beyond simple repair. If a church is significantly destroyed by war or arson, for example, its reconstruction calls for a rededication.

A church is desecrated when it suffers a crime, such as one committed against the eucharistic species, or that shows contempt for the church, or that offends the dignity of the person and society, such as a murder (CB 1070).

If a desecrated church is to be put to sacred use again, the bishop fittingly presides over the ceremony called Public Prayer after the Desecration of a Church (CB 1070–92). Acts of penitence are performed by the faithful, even though they are victims, not perpetrators, of the actions that offended their community. A special penitential rite may take place within Mass or within a celebration of the Word. After this, the building and altar may return to the regular celebration of the Mass.

If a church is closed permanently and then repurposed for secular use, it loses its dedication.[51] If a dedicated altar survives the destruction or repurposing of the church, it retains its dedicated status.[52] Such an altar may go back to a sacred use within the same building or as part of another church.

The elaborate ceremonies of dedication demonstrate that these structures enjoy a single sacred purpose. If that purpose is broken, a special ceremony restores it. At the beginning of their service, churches and altars are anointed with the same oil administered on human beings at sacraments that impart an indelible character: sacred chrism.

51. Canon 1212.
52. Canon 1238 §2.

Conclusion

The Care of Oils

The Gremial and Handwashing

Before pouring chrism at an ordination and at the dedication of a church and an altar, the bishop usually puts on a liturgical apron called a gremial. This protects the vestments he wears for the celebration. After any anointing, he washes his hands. These actions show the supplemental care given to the administration of the most sacred oil.

At the dedication of a church, the items prepared in advance include "a linen gremial" as well as "a basin and a pitcher of water, towels, and what is necessary for washing the hands of the Bishop and Priests who have anointed the walls of the church" (ODC chap. II, 21b). Commonly, a lemon is prepared in advance to help dissolve the oil in the water. The lemon works best if it has been halved across its equator and then seeded. Alternatively, a dishwashing soap may suffice.

During the dedication ceremony, the gremial pertains more to anointing the altar than the walls. The bishop may remove his chasuble before putting on the gremial (ODC chap. II, 63; chap. IV, 23), which will free his arms to reach around the altar top and perform the necessary actions. Only the bishop wears a gremial, but all who assist in anointing the walls need to wash their hands at its conclusion.

After the anointing, the bishop goes to the presider's chair where ministers bring him the items necessary for washing. He cleans his hands, removes the gremial, and again puts on his chasuble (ODC chap. II, 65; CB 904). Priests needing to wash up more commonly go to the credence table or an auxiliary space where the necessary items await them.

For the ordination of priests, the gremial is also prepared ahead of time together with the items needed for the bishop and the candidates to wash their hands (OBP 115c, e, 145; CB 520c, e). After the new priests have been vested, they approach the bishop for the anointing. He receives the gremial and anoints the palms of their hands. Then they all wash up (OBP 133, 161; CB 535).

At the ordination of a bishop, the gremial is also prepared (CB 568c), together with what is needed for washing hands (OBP 28c, e). After the prayer of consecration, the presiding bishop puts on the gremial to pour chrism on the head of the new bishop. Afterwards, the presiding bishop washes his hands (OBP 49; CB 586). There is no provision for the new bishop to wash his hands, presumably because they are not involved in the anointing. However, since oil was poured onto his head, he may appreciate the provision of some cloth afterwards.

At confirmation, a bishop usually does not wear the gremial because he stands to administer the sacrament, and he usually anoints the forehead only with the quantity of oil that adheres to his thumb. However, when the bishop finishes anointing all the candidates, he washes his hands. If any priests have assisted him, they do the same (CB 468).

If the anointing of the sick takes place in a common ceremony, the gremial is not used. Yet the bishop and the priests who assist him similarly wash their hands at its conclusion (CB 657).

Incense at the Close of the Chrism Mass

At the end of the chrism Mass, after the bishop gives the final blessing, the thurifer presents the censer to him. The bishop imposes incense on the burning coals (OBO 27). Normally a bishop or priest blesses the rising smoke with his hand, saying nothing, but the rubrics are silent about that in this case, probably because the bishop has just blessed the entire assembly.

The thurifer then leads the procession out of the church, followed by the crossbearer and those who are carrying the newly blessed and consecrated oils (OBO 27; CB 293). The hymn that accompanied the procession of the oils into the church, "O Redeemer," may be repeated at the end.

Although one may see incense at the end of any Mass, the rubrics do not call for it. Incense leads the procession into a church (GIRM 276a), but it does not lead the procession out. On the way in, incense leads the way because the presider needs it immediately for the cross and the altar (276b). However, at the end of a typical Mass, there is nothing left to incense. The procession exits without it.

The chrism Mass, of course, is not a typical Mass. The carrying of the vessels of oil suggests the first stage of their journey from the cathedral into the parishes and the hands of the priests who will use them. Incense especially prepares the path for the chrism, which has been not blessed, but consecrated. Incense precedes the chrism out of respect for the sacredness of this oil.

Interestingly, the only other Mass that concludes with a procession led by incense is the Mass of the Lord's Supper on Holy Thursday. That Mass ceases with the prayer after communion when a procession forms to carry the Blessed Sacrament to its place of reposition. Because the procession includes consecrated hosts, incense leads the way. The traditional occasion for the chrism Mass is the morning of Holy Thursday, so the only two Masses that call for incense in the final procession were both assigned to the same day.

The Bishop's Instructions

At the end of the chrism Mass, as the procession leaves the cathedral, the bishop retires to the sacristy with the priests. Usually they share the joy of their friendship and ministry before saying goodbye. However, the rubrics envision something more: "In the vesting room it is appropriate for the Bishop to instruct the Priests about the manner in which the sacred Oils are to be treated, honored, and carefully stored" (OBO 28).

The chrism Mass is more than a friendly reunion. It is more than the blessing of oils. It sketches the relationship between the bishop and his priests. He provides the materials that they will need to carry on their ministry, which they conduct in his name. The bishop has led them and the community through the prayers over the oils and the celebration of the Eucharist. Now he entrusts the oils to the priests.

In practice, some priests may have other members of their staff or parishioners pick up the oils and transport them back to the parishes.

Somehow the oils have to get transferred from the large urns typically used for this celebration into containers suitable for the parishes, usually smaller jars, packaged in a way to facilitate their transport. Often a team of people take the urns to an adjacent area to conduct the process. This represents the beginning of the actions that will fulfill the bishop's instructions at the end of the chrism Mass. In many dioceses, volunteers begin immediately after the oils have been blessed, while the Mass continues. They leave behind in the sanctuary some ceremonial vessels for the view of the faithful and the final procession led by the incense.

The bishop instructs the priests concerning how the oils are to be "treated, honored, and carefully stored." They are holy oils and deserve a proper place of reposition called an ambry. A priest or deacon may bless a new one following the Order for the Blessing of a Repository for the Holy Oils in chapter 32 of the Book of Blessings. In times past the ambry was commonly located in the sacristy of churches, accessible to the priest on the occasions when he needed to retrieve the oils, especially for baptisms and anointing the sick. Sometimes these oils rested in a nondescript box recessed in the sacristy wall. Today it is more common to have the ambry on view somewhere inside the parish church—the sanctuary, the baptistry, the nave or entry area, for example. The vessels may be on open display or secured inside a box walled in glass to facilitate visibility and accessibility during a public liturgy. Such housing will provide the honor that the bishop requests.

The oils should also be stored in a way that they do not spoil. The containers should be secure so that no impurities soil their contents—no dust, bugs, or mold. Priests usually store one container of the oil of the sick in their cars, to increase its availability in times of necessity. Even there, the container should be clean and stored reverently. If he uses the small metal containers called stocks, he should also store these with care to avoid leakage or disrespect. The introduction to the order for anointing the sick reminds priests to store the oil in a place of honor, keep it suitable for use, and replace it each year or more frequently (AS 22; PCS 22). Apparently, some priests who keep the oil in their cars have been negligent of these matters.

If the bishop gives instructions, he may consider these points:

- Take all the oil needed, but not an excessive amount.

- Carry the oils carefully and honorably from the cathedral to the parish.

- At an appropriate moment, present the oils inside the parish church.

- Replace the old oils with the new, disposing of the old in an appropriate way.

- Keep the new oils in a place of honor, securely sealed.

- Use the oils for the benefit of the people of God whenever celebrating the apposite sacraments.

The bishop may not be able to announce these points in person. Sometimes the end of the chrism Mass is a frenzy of farewells. However, he has other means of communicating with his priests about the proper treatment of the oils, especially through electronic messages or a printed card that each could receive together with his oils.

These instructions fulfill a brief note in the Code of Canon Law that the pastor is to obtain the oils from his own bishop and keep them carefully and fittingly.[1]

The Reception of the Oils

The parishes are to receive the oils after the chrism Mass. The Roman Missal provides a brief instruction at the conclusion of the rubrics for the celebration: "The reception of the Holy Oils may take place in individual parishes either before the celebration of the Evening Mass of the Lord's Supper or

---

1. Canon 847 §2.

at another time that seems more appropriate" (The Chrism Mass 15).

Some parishes have turned this into a ceremony. The United States Conference of Catholic Bishops even provides a template for one on its website.[2] It evolved from an order of service that the Vatican approved for the United States in 1989. The original version envisioned the presentation of the oils during the procession of the gifts at a Mass in the parish, such as that of the Lord's Supper on Holy Thursday. This imitated the way that ministers present the oils at the chrism Mass. However, wisely, this is no longer suggested. At the chrism Mass, the unblessed oils are presented together with the bread and wine because all these elements will be blessed and consecrated. In the parishes, the blessing and consecration has already taken place, so the oils are no longer part of the offering of the people of God within a celebration of the Eucharist. The parish is receiving what was previously offered, blessed, and consecrated.

Therefore, the USCCB recommends that the oils be placed on a table before the beginning of a Mass, whether it be Holy Thursday or another day. Then, after the sign of the cross and the greeting, the priest may catechize the people about the use of the three oils. Each is then placed in its repository, possibly an ambry in view of the faithful, and the Mass continues as usual.

The missal says that the occasion may be the Mass of the Lord's Supper, but it need not be. If the chrism Mass has taken place on Tuesday of Holy Week, for example, the parish could receive the oils during the Wednesday daily Mass.

---

2. Order for the Reception of the Holy Oils, https://www.usccb.org /prayer-and-worship/liturgical-year-and-calendar/triduum/order-for-the -reception-of-the-holy-oils.

This would put them on display and make them ready for immediate use.

However, the missal does not really specify what "reception" means. Does it mean a ceremony? Or does it simply mean that someone from the diocesan office delivers the oils to the parish office, where the secretary "receives" them at the front door? Parishes have considerable latitude how to receive the oils, but they may wish to take advantage of an opportunity to highlight their purpose in the presence of the people.

If the cathedral is itself a parish, it makes little sense to have a reception of the oils there. The cathedral is probably the building where the oils became holy, and they traveled nowhere to arrive in their place.

Handling the Vessels

The care of the oils is also demonstrated by the handling of the vessels during the ceremonies. During the chrism Mass, ministers bring large vessels of oil to the bishop (OBO 16–22). Lay ministers may carry those to be blessed for the sick and the catechumens, as well as the vessel of fragrance, but only deacons carry the oil to be consecrated for chrism (OBO 16). At the end of the chrism Mass, each is carried ceremoniously in the final procession (OBO 27). They are then to be carefully transported to the parish churches.[3]

At a confirmation liturgy, when the moment comes for the bishop to administer the sacrament, a deacon presents him with the vessel of chrism (OConf 26). If the number of those to be confirmed is so great that priests will assist in administering the sacrament, the deacon presents all the vessels of chrism to the bishop, and the bishop gives each

---

3. OBO 28; Roman Missal, The Chrism Mass 15.

priest the vessel he needs (OConf 28; CB 465). These actions show the sacredness of the chrism, consecrated by the bishop, who personally places it into the hands of his priests. At the consecration of a church, when the moment arrives for the anointing, a deacon or another minister carries the chrism to the bishop. If other priests assist him in anointing the walls, the bishop hands them their vessels (ODC chap. II, 63; CB 902). If he is anointing a new altar in a church that has already been dedicated, he receives the chrism from a deacon or another minister (ODC chap. IV, 49). In this case, he does not share the anointing with priests because only the altar, not the walls, are to be anointed.

When a priest presides for the sacraments of initiation, for example at the Easter Vigil, he confirms the adults he baptizes. In this case, someone presents him with the vessel of chrism just before the confirmation (OCIA 231; RCIA 235). Traditionally, this task would be performed by a deacon, but sometimes a parish has no deacon, and a layperson fulfills the role.

When the bishop presides for a communal celebration of the anointing of the sick, the ministers follow a similar practice. A deacon brings the bishop the vessel or vessels with the blessed oil. If priests are to assist him, the bishop hands each priest the vessel he will use (CB 655). The priests receive their vessels not from the deacon, which would seem easier, but from the bishop, which seems more intentional. The simple gesture reminds the priest that each time he anoints the sick, he assists the bishop's ministry.

The priest who anoints the sick usually brings the vessel with him to the sick person's side. He may retrieve it from the ambry at church or from a secure place in his own car.[4]

---

4. Canon 1003 §3.

The vessel should be of suitable material kept clean, and it holds oil of sufficient quantity absorbed into a cotton ball for ease of transport, safekeeping, and administration (AS 22; PCS 22).

These instructions show the care that the rubrics give to the handling of the vessels of oil, especially of those that hold sacred chrism.

Replacing the Oil

After the chrism Mass, priests may hear their bishop instruct them to replace their old oils with these new ones. He implies that the previous year's oils are to be disposed of in a worthy manner.

Instructions for disposing of oil appear only in the introduction to the order of anointing the sick. Sometimes a priest who has none of the oil blessed by the bishop blesses his own oil within the rite. However, this sometimes results in him having more blessed oil than he needs. He is not to keep the remaining oil that he blessed. He may use that oil only for that single instance. Consequently, the rubrics instruct him to absorb what remains of the blessed oil with cotton and to burn it in fire (AS 22; PCS 22).

The Book of Blessings 1127 calls for a similar procedure to dispose of old oils when the priest receives the new ones from the bishop. The priest, sacristan, or another person may absorb what remains in cotton, and then set the cotton on fire in a safe environment. Cotton takes a while to burn, so the person who accepts this responsibility best keeps an eye on the process. The burning may take place in a thurible, for example, or even as part of the fire that opens the Easter Vigil. In open spaces where fires are permitted, someone could reverently bring the old oil to be consumed by a fire prepared on the ground in the open air. However it is done, it would be appropriate for those burning the old oil to pray for the bishop, the priests, and all the people who participated in the administration of the full quantity of this oil over the past year.

Abbreviations and Colors

Traditionally the oils are kept in vessels marked with initials to indicate their contents. Whoever prepares these needs to take great care that each oil is poured into its proper vessel.

The oil of the sick is usually kept in a vessel marked OI, an abbreviation of the Latin words *oleum infirmorum*, meaning "the oil of those who are sick." One might expect the initials to read OS for the sake of the English translation. It is possible that a vessel has been prepared that way, but it is not likely because it will cause confusion.

Instead, the oil of catechumens sometimes rests in a vessel marked OS, as an abbreviation of *oleum sanctum* or "holy oil." In the past this was known as the oil of exorcism, so it is possible that one would find a vessel marked OE. It is even possible to carry the initials OC, which abbreviate the Latin words for the oil of catechumens: *oleum catechumenorum*.

Sacred chrism is most often kept in a vessel marked SC, indicating the Latin words *sacrum Chrisma*. One needs to be careful not to assume that OC stands for "the oil of chrism." It usually does not; OC usually designates the oil of catechumens. Chrism is the most sacred of the oils, and it has the most unique of the abbreviations.

A priest or deacon about to use the oil of chrism can perform a simple check to ensure that the vessel holds the correct contents: he removes the lid and smells the oil. The perfume is all the evidence he needs.

Traditionally, certain colors have been associated with these oils: violet for the oil of the sick because of the forgiveness of sins conferred with this sacrament; green for the oil of catechumens, suggesting the new life coming to those who will be baptized; and white for sacred chrism, the cause for celebration on festive occasions such as baptism, confirmation, the ordination of priests and bishops, and the dedication of churches and altars. Ribbons or cloths of such colors could still fittingly adorn the vessels stored in an ambry.

These designations and traditions help the faithful appreciate these oils.

Oils Past and Present

In biblical times oil was as common as water, bread, and wine. Oil delighted people in both the Old and New Testaments. In the most popular of the psalms, the Lord as shepherd provides an overflowing cup and anoints one's head with oil (23:5). Another psalm compares friendship with oil cascading pleasantly down one's head (133:2). Jesus advised his followers to conceal their fasting humbly by anointing their heads (Matt 6:17). In one of his parables, the Good Samaritan compassionately poured oil onto the wounds of an assault victim (Luke 10:34).

The Bible also confronts the misuse of oil. As deceitful speech even today is sometimes called "oily," so the psalmist knows a traitorous companion whose words were smoother than oil (Ps 55:22). Another psalm seeks retribution upon one who has cursed, hoping that the hurtful words sink like oil into the bones of the one who spoke them (109:18). Still another psalm chants that the oil of the wicked will never touch the singer's head (141:5).

Evidence for the commercial importance of oil comes from Jesus' parable of the dishonest steward, who helps his master's client cleverly falsify a ticket for one hundred measures of oil (Luke 16:6). The book of Revelation knew a time when famine destroyed the grain harvest but spared the source for oil (6:6). One sign of Babylon's fall, however, was the absence of oil from its market (Rev 18:13).

Twice the Acts of the Apostles hails Jesus as God's anointed (4:27; 10:38). Yet the women who intended to anoint Jesus after his death could not complete their mission at the empty tomb.[5] Those who follow him are called Christians, anointed ones, who receive anointing at their initiation. Like the wise virgins in another parable, Christians keep the grace of this oil ready at every hour, day and night (Matt 25:4).

In the ambry they sit, seemingly inert yet full of life; simple in their presentation yet beautiful in their application; situated locally in the parish church yet coming from the bishop's solemn ceremony at the cathedral; substances of nature yet promises of the supernatural. To the uncatechized they may seem like ordinary jars, but to the people of God they hold sacred oils.

---

5. Mark 16:1, for example.